Taste of Home
Chocolate
DELIGHTS

201 BROWNIES TRUFFLES, CAKES & MORE

TASTE OF HOME BOOKS • RDA ENTHUSIAST BRANDS, LLC • MILWAUKEE, WI

Taste*of*Home. Reader's digest

A TASTE OF HOME/READER'S DIGEST BOOK

EDITORIAL

Editor-in-Chief: Catherine Cassidy
Creative Director: Howard Greenberg
Editorial Operations Director: Kerri Balliet

Managing Editor/Print & Digital Books: Mark Hagen
Associate Creative Director: Edwin Robles Jr.

Associate Editor: Molly Jasinski
Art Director: Raeann Sundholm
Layout Designer: Nancy Novak
Editorial Production Manager: Dena Ahlers
Editorial Production Coordinator: Jill Banks
Copy Chief: Deb Warlaumont Mulvey
Contributing Copy Editor: Valerie Phillips
Editorial Intern: Michael Welch

Food Editors: Gina Nistico; James Schend;
Peggy Woodward, RD
Recipe Editors: Mary King; Irene Yeh
Business Analyst, Content Tools: Amanda Harmatys
Content Operations Assistant: Shannon Stroud
Editorial Services Administrator: Marie Brannon

Test Kitchen & Food Styling Manager:
Sarah Thompson
Test Cooks: Nicholas Iverson (Lead),
Matthew Hass, Lauren Knoelke
Food Stylists: Kathryn Conrad (Lead),
Shannon Roum, Leah Rekau
Prep Cooks: Bethany Van Jacobson (Lead), Megumi
Garcia, Melissa Hansen
Culinary Team Assistant: Megan Behr

Photography Director: Stephanie Marchese
Photographers: Dan Roberts, Jim Wieland
Photographer/Set Stylist: Grace Natoli Sheldon
Set Stylists: Melissa Franco, Stacey Genaw,
Dee Dee Jacq
Photo Studio Assistant: Ester Robards

Editorial Business Manager: Kristy Martin
Editorial Business Associate: Samantha Lea Stoeger

Editor, *Taste of Home*: Jeanne Ambrose
Associate Creative Director, *Taste of Home*:
Erin Burns
Art Director, *Taste of Home*: Kristin Bowker

BUSINESS

Vice President, Group Publisher: Kirsten Marchioli

Publisher, Taste of Home: Donna Lindskog

General Manager, Taste of Home Cooking School:
Erin Puariea

**Executive Producer, Taste of Home Online Cooking
School:** Karen Berner

THE READER'S DIGEST ASSOCIATION, INC.

President and Chief Executive Officer:
Bonnie Kintzer
**Vice President, Chief Operating Officer,
North America:** Howard Halligan
Chief Revenue Officer: Richard Sutton
Chief Marketing Officer: Leslie Dukker Doty
**Senior Vice President, Global HR &
Communications:** Phyllis E. Gebhardt, SPHR
**Vice President, Digital Content & Audience
Development:** Diane Dragan
Vice President, Brand Marketing: Beth Gorry
Vice President, Financial Planning & Analysis:
William Houston
Publishing Director, Books: Debra Polansky
Chief Technology Officer: Aneel Tejwaney
Vice President, Consumer Marketing Planning:
Jim Woods

For other Taste of Home books and products,
visit us at tasteofhome.com.

For more Reader's Digest products and information,
visit rd.com (in the United States) or rd.ca (in Canada).

International Standard Book Number:
978-1-61765-495-4
Library of Congress Control Number:
2015948971

Cover Photographer: Dan Roberts
Set Stylist: Dee Dee Jacq
Food Stylist: Shannon Roum

Pictured on front cover:
Irish Creme Chocolate Trifle, page 155
Pictured on back cover:
Valentine Heart Brownies, page 29, and
Brownie Cheesecake Snickers Pie, page 88
Illustrations on inside cover:
primiaou/Shutterstock.com

Printed in China.
3 5 7 9 10 8 6 4 2

LIKE US
facebook.com/tasteofhome

TWEET US
@tasteofhome

FOLLOW US
pinterest.com/taste_of_home

SHOP WITH US
shoptasteofhome.com

SHARE A RECIPE
tasteofhome.com/submit

Chocolate Glaze for Doughnuts, page 196
Hazelnut Mocha Coffee, page 175

TABLE OF CONTENTS

Coconut Bonbons, page 15

Chocolate Sauce, page 195

INDULGE IN CHOCOLATY GOODNESS

When it's time for dessert, one word comes to mind— chocolate. There's so much to love about this favorite treat, and *Taste of Home Chocolate Delights* offers 201 ways to enjoy it!

From cupcakes to brownies and from cake pops to truffles, the recipes found here offer chocolate in all its glory... including cheesecakes, cookies, trifles, sauces and more.

Try this **Simple Turtle Cheesecake,** page 148.

The most cherished cookbooks are filled with handwritten notes, and the "Baking Morsels" sprinkled throughout the book are the perfect places to jot down hints to share with your family. Combine time together in the kitchen with some chocolaty treats, and you have a sweet recipe for wonderful memories!

Chocolate Facts

Chocolate comes from cocoa beans, which are processed to produce cocoa powder, cocoa butter and chocolate liquor. Chocolate liquor is simply the liquid that's created when the meat of the cocoa bean nibs are crushed. **Here's the chocolaty difference in popular baking ingredients:**

BAKING COCOA is a powdery residue that remains after the cocoa butter is removed from the chocolate liquor. Dutch-processed cocoa has been treated during processing with an alkalizing agent, which produces a smoother flavor and darker color than untreated baking cocoa.

CANDY COATING is not considered true chocolate because it uses other vegetable fats instead of cocoa butter. Candy coatings come in a variety of flavors, and are used mainly as a coating on cookies, fruits or nuts, or in candy-making.

CHOCOLATE CHIPS are available in standard, miniature and larger "chunk" sizes. Chocolate chips come in a variety of flavors, including semisweet, milk, and vanilla or white.

CHOCOLATE SYRUP is a liquid made from cocoa, corn syrup and flavorings.

GERMAN SWEET CHOCOLATE comes in a bar and is a sweeter chocolate than semisweet.

MILK CHOCOLATE contains cocoa butter, sugar, vanilla, chocolate liquor and 12% milk solids. It's sold as chips and candy bars.

SEMISWEET AND BITTERSWEET CHOCOLATE are sometimes used interchangeably in cooking. However, bittersweet chocolate is less sweet than semisweet chocolate. Semisweet chocolate is made with chocolate liquor, additional cocoa butter, sugar and vanilla. It's sold as chips, in packages of 1-ounce squares, and as candy bars.

UNSWEETENED CHOCOLATE may also be called baking chocolate. It's solidified chocolate liquor and does not contain sugar. It's available in 1-ounce squares.

WHITE CHOCOLATE is not a true chocolate because it does not contain chocolate liquor. White chocolate is made with cocoa butter, sugar, milk solids and vanilla. It's available in packages of chips and 1-ounce squares.

Chocolate-Topped
Marshmallow Sticks

Candies,
Fudge & More

CHOCOLATE-TOPPED MARSHMALLOW STICKS

I like to use all sorts of different marshmallow shapes and flavors to mix this recipe up a bit. These fun sticks are quite popular at our local bake sales.

—TERI RASEY CADILLAC, MI

PREP: 20 MIN. + STANDING
COOK: 10 MIN. • **MAKES:** 3 DOZEN

- 2 **cups (12 ounces) semisweet chocolate chips**
- 3 **teaspoons shortening, divided**
- 36 **lollipop sticks**
- 1 **package (10 ounces) large marshmallows (about 36)**
- ½ **cup white baking chips**
   Optional toppings: assorted nonpareils, colored sugars, small or crushed candies and flaked coconut

1. In a microwave, melt chocolate chips and 2 teaspoons shortening; stir until smooth.
2. Insert one lollipop stick into each marshmallow. Dip marshmallows in melted chocolate, turning to coat; allow excess to drip off. Place on waxed paper.
3. In a microwave, melt white baking chips with remaining shortening; drizzle over chocolate. Decorate with toppings if desired. Let stand until set.
4. Use to stir servings of hot cocoa. Store in an airtight container.

> ### CANDY CRUSHING
> Crush up hard candies by placing them inside a heavy-duty resealable plastic bag and using a hammer.

NUTTY CHOCOLATE PEANUT CLUSTERS

I'm always amazed at just how simple these chocolaty nut clusters are to make. Bring them out after holiday meals or for a party.

—CHRISTINE EILERTS JONES, OK

PREP: 10 MIN. + CHILLING
COOK: 10 MIN. • **MAKES:** 2¾ POUNDS

- 1 **pound white candy coating, chopped**
- 2 **cups (12 ounces) semisweet chocolate chips**
- 1 **jar (16 ounces) dry roasted peanuts**

1. In a double boiler or metal bowl over hot water, melt candy coating and chocolate chips; stir until smooth. Remove from the heat; stir in peanuts.
2. Drop by rounded teaspoonfuls onto waxed paper-lined baking sheets. Refrigerate clusters for 10-15 minutes or until set. Store in airtight containers.

PEANUT BUTTER CHOCOLATE CUPS

Our children love these creamy candies. I think they're even better than the store-bought ones.
—ALJENE WENDLING SEATTLE, WA

PREP: 20 MIN. + CHILLING
MAKES: 1 DOZEN

> 1 milk chocolate candy bar (7 ounces)
> ¼ cup butter
> 1 tablespoon shortening
> ¼ cup creamy peanut butter

1. In a microwave, melt chocolate, butter and shortening; stir until smooth. Place foil or paper miniature baking cups in a miniature muffin tin. Place 1 tablespoon of chocolate mixture in each cup.
2. In a microwave, melt peanut butter; stir until smooth. Spoon into cups. Top with the remaining chocolate mixture. Remelt chocolate mixture if necessary. Refrigerate 30 minutes or until firm.

CHOCOLATE CARAMEL CRACKER BARS

Make them Saturday and they'll be gone by Monday—these bars with a cracker crust are just that delicious. Treat your family to the yumminess!
—ALLY BILLHORN WILTON, IA

PREP: 15 MIN. • **COOK:** 10 MIN. + CHILLING
MAKES: 27 BARS

> 1 teaspoon plus ¾ cup butter, cubed
> 45 Club crackers (2½x1 inch)
> 1 can (14 ounces) sweetened condensed milk
> ½ cup packed brown sugar
> 3 tablespoons light corn syrup
> 1 cup (6 ounces) semisweet chocolate chips

1. Line a 9-in. square baking pan with foil and grease the foil with 1 teaspoon butter. Arrange a single layer of the crackers in the pan.
2. In a large saucepan, combine milk, brown sugar, corn syrup and remaining butter. Bring to a boil over medium heat, stirring occasionally. Reduce heat to maintain a low boil; cook and stir 7 minutes. Remove from heat. Evenly spread a third of the mixture over the crackers. Repeat cracker and caramel layers twice.
3. Immediately sprinkle chocolate chips over caramel; let stand for 3-5 minutes or until glossy. Spread over top. Cover and refrigerate 2 hours or until chocolate is set. Using foil, lift layers out of pan; cut into 3x1-in. bars.

CHOCOLATE-DIPPED LAVENDER PINE NUT BRITTLE

Take a trip to the south of France with this uniquely flavored brittle. It's a lovely addition to any candy spread.

—TASTE OF HOME TEST KITCHEN

PREP: 15 MIN. • **COOK:** 25 MIN.
MAKES: 3 POUNDS

- 1 **tablespoon butter, melted**
- 3 **cups sugar**
- 1 **cup light corn syrup**
- ½ **cup water**
- 4½ **cups pine nuts**
- ¼ **cup butter, softened**
- 2 **teaspoons baking soda**
- 2 **teaspoons vanilla extract**
- 1 **teaspoon dried lavender flowers**
- ½ **teaspoon salt**
- 1 **pound dark chocolate candy coating, coarsely chopped**

1. Grease two 15x10x1-in. pans with melted butter; set aside.

2. In a large saucepan, combine the sugar, corn syrup and water. Cook without stirring over medium heat until a candy thermometer reads 230° (thread stage). Carefully add pine nuts; cook and stir constantly until mixture reaches 300° (hard-crack stage).

3. Remove from the heat; stir in the softened butter, baking soda, vanilla, lavender and salt. Immediately pour into prepared pans. Spread to ¼-in. thickness. Cool before breaking into pieces.

4. In a microwave, melt chocolate coating; stir until smooth. Dip each candy piece halfway into the melted chocolate; allow excess to drip off. Place on waxed paper and let stand until set. Store in an airtight container.

NOTES *Look for dried lavender flowers in spice shops. If using lavender from the garden, make sure it hasn't been treated with chemicals.*

We recommend you test your candy thermometer before each use by bringing water to a boil; the thermometer should read 212°. Adjust your recipe temperature up or down based on your test.

BAKING MORSELS

Chocolate-Dipped
Candy Canes

CHOCOLATE-DIPPED CANDY CANES

I couldn't resist combining my two loves—peppermint and chocolate! If any candy canes break accidentally, it's an extra treat for you!
—SANDRA BAUMGARTEN VANCOUVER, WA

PREP: 20 MIN. + STANDING
COOK: 5 MIN. • **MAKES:** 1 DOZEN

- **1 cup semisweet chocolate chips**
- **12 candy canes (6 inches each)**
- **3 ounces white baking chocolate, chopped**
- **Optional toppings: assorted colored sugars or sprinkles and crushed candies**

1. In a microwave, melt chocolate chips; stir until smooth. Dip curved ends of candy canes in chocolate; allow excess to drip off. Place candy canes on waxed paper.

2. In a microwave, melt white baking chocolate; stir until smooth. Drizzle over chocolate. Decorate with toppings if desired. Let stand until set.

3. Use to stir servings of hot cocoa.

CANDY CREATION

Candy canes are said to have been the idea of a choirmaster at a cathedral in Germany in the 1670s. He bent the end of a piece of sugar stick candy to resemble a shepherd's staff. The canes were handed out to children to help keep them quiet during the long Christmas services. Stripes did not appear until after 1900.

CANDY-LICIOUS FUDGE

A no-fuss fudge prepared in the microwave that tastes like a candy bar? It sounds too good to be true, but it's not!
—DEE LANCASTER OZARK, MO

PREP: 15 MIN. + CHILLING
MAKES: 2¼ POUNDS

- **1 teaspoon butter**
- **1 can (14 ounces) sweetened condensed milk**
- **1 package (11 ounces) peanut butter and milk chocolate chips**
- **1 cup milk chocolate chips**
- **⅔ cup milk chocolate English toffee bits**
- **1 cup chopped pecans**
- **2 teaspoons vanilla extract**

Line a 9-in. square baking pan with foil and grease the foil with butter; set aside. In a large microwave-safe bowl, combine the milk, chips and toffee bits. Microwave, uncovered, on high for 1 minute; stir. Cook 1-2 minutes longer, stirring every minute, or until chips are melted. Stir in pecans and vanilla. Transfer to prepared pan. Cover and refrigerate for at least 1 hour. Using foil, lift fudge out of pan. Gently peel off foil; cut into 1-in. squares. Store in an airtight container.

NOTE *This recipe was tested in a 1,100-watt microwave.*

CRANBERRY-PISTACHIO TRUFFLES

Rich and encrusted with pistachios, these cranberry-studded truffles are too good to pass up. They're a favorite indulgence at Christmastime.

—MICHAEL JONES YORKTOWN, VA

PREP: 35 MIN. + CHILLING
MAKES: ABOUT 2½ DOZEN

- 10 ounces 53% cacao dark baking chocolate, chopped
- ¾ cup whole-berry cranberry sauce
- 2 tablespoons plus 1½ teaspoons heavy whipping cream
- 2 tablespoons confectioners' sugar
- 2 tablespoons dark baking cocoa
- ½ cup finely chopped shelled pistachios

1. Place chocolate in a small bowl. In a small saucepan, bring cranberry sauce and cream just to a boil. Pour over chocolate; whisk until smooth. Cool to room temperature, stirring occasionally. Cover and refrigerate for 3 hours or until firm enough to shape.

2. Combine confectioners' sugar and cocoa. Shape truffle mixture into 1-in. balls. Roll in cocoa mixture, then in pistachios. Store truffles in an airtight container in the refrigerator.

TIGER BUTTER CANDY

PREP: 15 MIN. + CHILLING
MAKES: ABOUT 1¼ POUNDS

- 1 pound white candy coating, coarsely chopped
- ½ cup chunky peanut butter
- ½ cup semisweet chocolate chips
- ½ teaspoon shortening

Line a 15x10x1-in. pan with foil; set aside. In a microwave-safe bowl, melt candy coating and peanut butter; stir until smooth. Spread into prepared pan. In another microwave-safe bowl, melt chocolate chips and shortening; stir until smooth. Drizzle over top; cut through with a knife to swirl. Chill until firm. Break into pieces. Store in an airtight container.

> Fans of tiger butter fudge will revel in this version that's very similar to bark candy. The chocolate swirls are pleasing to the eye, and the creamy peanut butter flavor is an added delight.
>
> **—PHILIP JONES** LUBBOCK, TX

TRUFFLE CHERRIES

My family and I are a bunch of chocolate lovers. Double chocolate gems like these don't last long at our house!

—**ANNE DROUIN** DUNNVILLE, ON

PREP: 20 MIN. + CHILLING
MAKES: ABOUT 2 DOZEN

- ⅓ **cup heavy whipping cream**
- 2 **tablespoons butter**
- 2 **tablespoons sugar**
- 4 **ounces semisweet chocolate, chopped**
- 1 **jar (8 ounces) maraschino cherries with stems, well drained**

COATING

- 6 **ounces semisweet chocolate, chopped**
- 2 **tablespoons shortening**

1. In a small saucepan, bring the cream, butter and sugar to a boil, stirring constantly. Remove from the heat; stir in chocolate until melted. Cover and refrigerate for at least 4 hours or until easy to handle.

2. Pat cherries with paper towels until very dry. Shape a teaspoonful of chocolate mixture around each cherry, forming a ball. Cover and refrigerate for 2-3 hours or until firm.

3. In a microwave, melt chocolate and shortening; stir until smooth. Dip cherries until coated; allow excess to drip off. Place on waxed paper to set.

SWEET & SALTY CANDY

I've been making this candy for the past few years to serve at teacher appreciation lunches and to contribute for bake sales. It always disappears quickly, no matter where I take it! For bake sales, I break the candy up and package it in little cellophane bags from the craft store.

—ANNA GINSBERG AUSTIN, TX

PREP: 15 MIN. **• BAKE:** 10 MIN. + COOLING
MAKES: ABOUT 1½ POUNDS

- **2 cups miniature pretzels, coarsely crushed**
- **½ cup corn chips, coarsely crushed**
- **½ cup salted peanuts**
- **½ cup butter, cubed**
- **½ cup packed brown sugar**
- **1½ cups semisweet chocolate chips**

1. Preheat oven to 350°. Line a 13x9-in. baking pan with foil and grease the foil; set aside. In a large bowl, combine the pretzels, corn chips and peanuts.

2. In a small saucepan, melt the butter. Stir in brown sugar until melted. Bring to a boil, stirring frequently. Boil 1 minute, stirring twice. Pour over pretzel mixture; toss to coat. Transfer mixture to prepared pan.

3. Bake 7 minutes. Sprinkle with chocolate chips. Bake 1-2 minutes longer or until chips are softened. Spread over top. Cool on a wire rack 1 hour. Break into pieces. Store in an airtight container.

BACKWOODS BONFIRE BARK

Packed with chocolate, marshmallows and peanuts, this treat reminds me of being up north at my family's cabin. The bark also sells quickly at school bake sales.
—**JAMIE MCMAHON** COLOGNE, MN

PREP: 10 MIN. • **COOK:** 5 MIN. + STANDING
MAKES: ABOUT 1½ POUNDS

- **1 pound semisweet chocolate, chopped**
- **1½ cups honey bear-shaped crackers**
- **1½ cups miniature marshmallows**
- **¾ cup dry roasted peanuts**

1. Place chocolate in a microwave-safe bowl. Microwave on high for 1 minute; stir. Microwave 1 minute longer in 20-second intervals until melted; stir until smooth.
2. Spread to ¼-in. thickness on a waxed paper-lined baking sheet. Immediately sprinkle crackers, marshmallows and peanuts over chocolate; press in lightly.
3. Chill until firm. Break or cut into pieces. Store in an airtight container.

A TOUCH OF SWEETNESS

Kick your bark up to a whole new sweet level by using honey-roasted peanuts in place of dry roasted peanuts in this recipe.

COCONUT BONBONS

I'll often top these bonbons with a mini sugar flower to match my party theme.
—**CLAUDIA RUISS** MASSAPEQUA, NY

PREP: 20 MIN. + CHILLING
MAKES: 2½ DOZEN

- **2⅔ cups flaked coconut, chopped**
- **⅔ cup confectioners' sugar**
- **½ cup sweetened condensed milk**
- **¼ cup finely chopped almonds, toasted**
- **2 tablespoons butter, softened**
- **½ teaspoon vanilla extract**
- **2 cups (12 ounces) semisweet chocolate chips**
- **1 tablespoon shortening**
  Colored jimmies or coarse sugar, optional

1. In a small bowl, combine the coconut, confectioners' sugar, milk, almonds, butter and vanilla. Cover and refrigerate for at least 2 hours.
2. Roll into 1-in. balls; place on waxed paper-lined pans. Refrigerate for at least 1 hour.
3. In a microwave, melt chocolate chips and shortening; stir until smooth. Dip balls in chocolate; allow excess to drip off. Return to waxed paper-lined pans. Sprinkle with jimmies or coarse sugar if desired. Refrigerate until firm.

Transfer to a resealable plastic freezer bag. May be frozen for up to 1 month. **TO USE FROZEN BALLS** *Thaw at room temperature.*

PEPPERMINT PATTIES

PREP: 25 MIN. + FREEZING
MAKES: ABOUT 12 DOZEN

- 3 **pounds confectioners' sugar**
- 1 **can (14 ounces) sweetened condensed milk**
- ½ **cup butter, melted**
- 3 **teaspoons peppermint extract**
- 3 **pounds milk chocolate candy coating, coarsely chopped**

1. In a large bowl, beat confectioners' sugar, milk, butter and extract until smooth. Shape into ½-in. balls and flatten into patties. Freeze 30 minutes.
2. In a microwave, melt half of candy coating at a time; dip patties into chocolate. Let excess drip off. Place on waxed paper-lined baking sheets until set. Store in airtight containers.

> Sometimes I'll add a few drops of green food coloring to the mixture before shaping the patties and dipping them in chocolate.
>
> **—MARY ESTER HOLLOWAY**
> BOWERSTON, OH

CRUNCHY CHOCOLATE MINT BALLS

Mom used to make these in advance so we'd have them for the holidays. We had an ice cream container full in the freezer, but they never lasted until Christmas Day. I now make them for my family. For a special touch, I place them in mini baking cups.
—AMANDA TRIFF DARTMOUTH, NS

PREP: 50 MIN. + FREEZING
MAKES: 4½ DOZEN

- 1 **package (10 ounces) mint chocolate chips**
- ¼ **cup butter, softened**
- 1 **can (14 ounces) sweetened condensed milk**
- 1¼ **cups chocolate wafer crumbs (about 22 wafers)**
  White jimmies

1. In a double boiler or metal bowl over hot water, melt chips and butter; stir until smooth. Stir in milk. Add wafer crumbs; mix to coat. Refrigerate for 1 hour or until easy to handle.
2. Roll into 1-in. balls; roll in jimmies. Place on a waxed paper-lined 15x10x1-in. baking pan; freeze until firm.

Peppermint Patties

WHITE CHOCOLATE LATTE CUPS

A smooth, rich caramel fills homemade chocolate cups for a decadent dessert. These are great for either entertaining or potlucks.

—*TASTE OF HOME* TEST KITCHEN

PREP: 30 MIN. • **COOK:** 20 MIN. + CHILLING
MAKES: 1½ DOZEN

- 1 **cup (6 ounces) dark chocolate chips**
- 2 **teaspoons shortening**

FILLING

- 3 **tablespoons sugar**
- ¾ **cup heavy whipping cream**
- ¼ **cup coffee liqueur**
- 1 **teaspoon instant espresso powder**
- 14 **ounces white baking chocolate, chopped**
  Chocolate-covered coffee beans

1. In a microwave, melt chocolate chips and shortening; stir until smooth. Using a narrow pastry brush, brush the inside of eighteen 2-in. foil muffin cup liners with ½ teaspoon melted chocolate. Refrigerate for 15 minutes or until firm. Repeat the layers twice. Chill until set.

2. In a large heavy skillet, cook sugar over medium-low heat until melted and a golden amber color. Gradually stir in cream; cook and stir until sugar is dissolved. Add liqueur and espresso powder; stir until smooth. Stir in white chocolate until melted. Transfer to a small bowl; cover and refrigerate for 1-2 hours or until slightly thickened.

3. Carefully remove and discard foil liners from chocolate cups. Spoon or pipe the filling into cups; garnish with coffee beans. Store in an airtight container in the refrigerator.

DELECTABLE MAPLE NUT CHOCOLATES

This recipe goes back about 40 years. My father loved anything with maple flavoring, so my mother tweaked a brownie recipe to suit his tastes. She would be so happy to know her recipe is still loved and shared after all these years.

—BETSY KING DULUTH, MN

PREP: 1 HOUR + CHILLING
MAKES: ABOUT 13 DOZEN

- 1 **can (14 ounces) sweetened condensed milk**
- ½ **cup butter, cubed**
- 7½ **cups confectioners' sugar**
- 2 **cups chopped walnuts**
- 2 **teaspoons maple flavoring**
- 1 **teaspoon vanilla extract**
- 4 **cups (24 ounces) semisweet chocolate chips**
- 2 **ounces bittersweet chocolate, chopped**
- 2 **teaspoons shortening**

1. In a small saucepan, combine milk and butter. Cook and stir over low heat until the butter is melted. Place the confectioners' sugar in a large bowl; add milk mixture and beat until smooth. Stir in the walnuts, maple flavoring and vanilla. Roll into ¾-in. balls; place on waxed paper-lined baking sheets. Refrigerate until firm, about 1 hour.

2. In a microwave, melt the chips, bittersweet chocolate and shortening; stir until smooth. Dip the balls into chocolate; allow excess to drip off. Place on waxed paper; let stand until set. Store in an airtight container.

FREEZE OPTION *Shape and freeze the balls of maple candy for up to 2 months if desired. Thaw candy before dipping into melted chocolate mixture.*

BAKING MORSELS

MICROWAVE MARSHMALLOW FUDGE

This foolproof fudge takes just four ingredients and 15 minutes, so it's excellent when time is short. It's so easy, you can fix it whenever you're craving a sweet treat. Use different flavors of frosting and chips for variety.

—**SUE ROSS** CASA GRANDE, AZ

PREP: 15 MIN. + CHILLING
MAKES: ABOUT 2 POUNDS

- 1 **teaspoon butter**
- 1 **can (16 ounces) chocolate frosting**
- 2 **cups (12 ounces) semisweet chocolate chips**
- ½ **cup chopped walnuts**
- ½ **cup miniature marshmallows**

1. Line a 9-in. square pan with foil and grease the foil with butter; set aside. In a microwave, melt frosting and chocolate chips; stir until smooth. Stir in walnuts; cool for 10 minutes. Stir in marshmallows. Transfer to prepared pan. Cover and refrigerate until firm.
2. Using foil, lift fudge out of pan. Discard foil; cut the fudge into 1-in. squares. Store in an airtight container in the refrigerator.

DARK CHOCOLATE RASPBERRY FUDGE

Something about the combination of dark chocolate and raspberry is so addicting. This fudge makes a heartfelt homemade gift, or just a treat that's worth sharing.

—**BARBARA LENTO** HOUSTON, PA

PREP: 15 MIN. + FREEZING
COOK: 5 MIN. + CHILLING
MAKES: 3 POUNDS (81 PIECES)

- 1 **package (10 to 12 ounces) white baking chips**
- 1 **teaspoon butter, softened**
- 3 **cups dark chocolate chips**
- 1 **can (14 ounces) sweetened condensed milk**
- ¼ **cup raspberry liqueur**
- ⅛ **teaspoon salt**

1. Place baking chips in a single layer on a small baking sheet. Freeze 30 minutes. Line a 9-in. square pan with foil; grease foil with butter.
2. In a large microwave-safe bowl, combine dark chocolate chips and milk. Microwave, uncovered, on high for 2 minutes; stir. Microwave in additional 30-second intervals, stirring until smooth. Stir in liqueur and salt. Add white baking chips; stir just until partially melted. Spread into prepared pan. Refrigerate 1 hour or until firm.
3. Using foil, lift fudge out of pan. Remove foil; cut the fudge into 1-in. squares. Store in an airtight container in the refrigerator.

CHOCOLATE CHERRY TRUFFLES

My cherry truffles were the delicious result of a kitchen experiment involving a bottle of kirsch I'd received as a gift and some dried cherries I had on hand. They won a blue ribbon at the Wisconsin State Fair!
—**GERRY COFTA** MILWAUKEE, WI

PREP: 1½ HOURS + STANDING
MAKES: 4 DOZEN

- 1 **cup finely chopped dried cherries**
- ¼ **cup cherry brandy**
- 11 **ounces 53% cacao dark baking chocolate, chopped**
- ½ **cup heavy whipping cream**
- 1 **teaspoon cherry extract**

COATING

- 4 **ounces milk chocolate, chopped**
- 4 **ounces dark chocolate, chopped**
  Melted dark, milk and white chocolate and pearl dust, optional

1. In a small bowl, combine cherries and brandy; cover and let soak for 1 hour or until cherries are softened.

2. Place dark chocolate in a small bowl. In a small saucepan, bring cream just to a boil. Pour over chocolate; whisk until smooth. Stir in extract and soaked cherries with liquid. Cool to room temperature, stirring occasionally. Refrigerate for 1 hour or until firm.

3. Shape into 1-in. balls. Place on baking sheets; cover and refrigerate for at least 1 hour.

4. In a microwave, melt the milk chocolate; stir until smooth. Dip half of the balls into milk chocolate, allowing excess to drip off. Place on waxed paper; let stand until set.

5. Melt dark chocolate; stir until smooth. Dip remaining balls into dark chocolate, allowing excess to drip off. Place on waxed paper; let stand until set. Drizzle with melted chocolate and decorate with pearl dust as desired. Store in an airtight container in the refrigerator.

NOTE *Pearl dust is available from Wilton Industries. Call 800-794-5866 or visit* wilton.com.

MACADAMIA NUT FUDGE

My aunt lives in Hawaii, and she keeps our family supplied with fresh pineapples, mangoes and macadamia nuts, as well as recipes like this one. My neighbors like this fudge so much that they have started calling me the Candy Lady of Cleveland.

—VICKI FIORANELLI CLEVELAND, MS

PREP: 15 MIN. + CHILLING
MAKES: ABOUT 5 POUNDS

- 2 teaspoons plus ½ cup butter, divided
- 4½ cups granulated sugar
- 1 can (12 ounces) evaporated milk
- 3 cups chopped macadamia nuts, divided
- 12 ounces German sweet chocolate, chopped
- 1 package (12 ounces) semisweet chocolate chips
- 1 jar (7 ounces) marshmallow creme
- 2 teaspoons vanilla extract
- ½ teaspoon salt, optional

1. Line two 9-in. square pans with foil; butter the foil with the 2 teaspoons butter. Set aside.
2. In a large heavy saucepan, combine the sugar, milk and remaining butter. Bring to a gentle boil. Cook for 5 minutes, stirring constantly. Remove from the heat; stir in 2 cups nuts, chopped chocolate, chocolate chips, marshmallow creme, vanilla and salt if desired.
3. Pour fudge into prepared pans; sprinkle remaining nuts over top and press in lightly. Refrigerate until firm. Using foil, lift fudge out of pans. Discard foil; cut fudge into 1-in. squares. Store in an airtight container.

PECAN NUT FUDGE *Use 3 cups of chopped toasted pecans in place of the macadamia nuts.*

Macadamia Nut Fudge

CHOCOLATE-COVERED ALMOND BUTTER BRICKLE

I love a soft butter brittle because the texture is wonderful and different, and the taste reminds me of a favorite candy bar.

—JOANN BELACK BRADENTON, FL

PREP: 10 MIN. • **COOK:** 20 MIN. + CHILLING
MAKES: ABOUT 1¾ POUNDS

- 1½ **teaspoons plus 2 tablespoons unsalted butter, divided**
- 1 **cup crunchy almond butter**
- ½ **teaspoon baking soda**
- 1 **teaspoon plus 2 tablespoons water, divided**
- ¾ **cup sugar**
- ¾ **cup light corn syrup**
- 1 **teaspoon almond extract**
- 1 **cup 60% cacao bittersweet chocolate baking chips**
- ⅓ **cup chopped almonds, toasted**
- ¾ **cup flaked coconut**

1. Grease a 15x10x1-in. pan with 1½ teaspoons butter. Place almond butter in a microwave-safe bowl; microwave, covered, at 50% power 30-60 seconds or until softened, stirring once. In a small bowl, dissolve baking soda in 1 teaspoon water. Set aside almond butter and baking soda mixture.

2. In a large heavy saucepan, combine sugar, corn syrup and 2 tablespoons water. Bring to a boil over medium heat, stirring constantly. Using a pastry brush dipped in water, wash down the sides of the pan to eliminate sugar crystals. Cook until a candy thermometer reads 240° (soft-ball stage), stirring occasionally, about 10 minutes. Add remaining butter; cook until candy thermometer reads 300° (hard-crack stage), stirring frequently, about 5 minutes longer.

3. Remove from heat; stir in the softened almond butter, almond extract and dissolved baking soda. (Candy will foam.) Immediately pour into prepared pan. Spread to ¼-in. thickness.

4. Sprinkle with chocolate chips; let stand until chocolate begins to melt. Spread evenly; sprinkle with almonds and coconut, pressing slightly to adhere. Cool slightly. Refrigerate 1 hour or until chocolate is set.

5. Break candy into pieces. Store between layers of waxed paper in an airtight container.

NOTE *To toast nuts, bake in a shallow pan in a 350° oven for 5-10 minutes or cook in a skillet over low heat until lightly browned, stirring occasionally.*

BAKING MORSELS

CHOCOLATE PEPPERMINT BARK

These treats are such a snap to make, I almost feel guilty serving them. But nobody seems to mind I didn't put in much effort—they just keep coming back for more.

—KESLIE HOUSER PASCO, WA

PREP: 15 MIN. + CHILLING
MAKES: ABOUT 1 POUND

- 6 **ounces white baking chocolate, chopped**
- 1 **cup crushed peppermint or spearmint candies, divided**
- 1 **cup (6 ounces) semisweet chocolate chips**

1. In a microwave, melt the white chocolate at 70% power; stir until smooth. Stir in ⅓ cup crushed candies. Repeat with chocolate chips and an additional ⅓ cup candies. Alternately drop spoonfuls of chocolate and white chocolate mixtures onto a waxed paper-lined baking sheet.

2. Using a metal spatula, cut through candy to swirl and spread to ¼-in. thickness. Sprinkle with remaining crushed candies.

3. Refrigerate until firm. Break into pieces. Store between layers of waxed paper in an airtight container.

PISTACHIO CRANBERRY BARK *Omit peppermint candies. Stir 3 tablespoons toasted chopped pistachios and 2 tablespoons dried cranberries into each bowl of melted chocolate. Proceed as directed. Sprinkle the top with 2 tablespoons toasted chopped pistachios and 2 tablespoons dried cranberries.*

NOTE *This recipe was tested in a 1,100-watt microwave.*

BRANDY ALEXANDER FUDGE

We love to indulge in this marbled fudge inspired by the popular brandy drink. My sister-in-law won first place with this recipe at the county fair.

—**DEBBIE NEUBAUER** PINE CITY, MN

PREP: 30 MIN.
COOK: 15 MIN. + CHILLING
MAKES: ABOUT 3 POUNDS

- 1 teaspoon plus ¾ cup butter, divided
- 3 cups sugar
- 1 can (5 ounces) evaporated milk
- 1 jar (7 ounces) marshmallow creme
- 1 cup (6 ounces) semisweet chocolate chips
- 2 tablespoons brandy
- 1 cup white baking chips
- 2 tablespoons creme de cacao or Kahlua (coffee liqueur)

1. Line an 8-in. square pan with foil and grease the foil with 1 teaspoon butter; set aside. In a large heavy saucepan, combine the sugar, milk and remaining butter. Bring to a full boil over medium heat, stirring constantly; cook and stir for 4 minutes. Remove from the heat and set aside.

2. Divide marshmallow creme between two small heat-resistant bowls. Pour half of the sugar mixture into each bowl. To one bowl, stir in semisweet chips until melted; stir in brandy. Into the remaining bowl, stir in white chips until melted; stir in creme de cacao.

3. Spread chocolate mixture into prepared pan. Top with white mixture; cut through with a knife to swirl. Cool to room temperature. Chill until set completely.

4. Using foil, lift fudge out of pan. Discard foil; cut the fudge into 1-in. squares. Store in an airtight container in the refrigerator.

NOTE *Once you add the chips to the mixture, work fast, as the fudge sets up quickly.*

COOKIE DOUGH TRUFFLES

The filling at the center of these candies tastes like actual chocolate chip cookie dough, without any of the worries associated with raw eggs.

—LANITA DEDON SLAUGHTER, LA

PREP: 1 HOUR + CHILLING
MAKES: 5½ DOZEN

- ½ **cup butter, softened**
- ¾ **cup packed brown sugar**
- 1 **teaspoon vanilla extract**
- 2 **cups all-purpose flour**
- 1 **can (14 ounces) sweetened condensed milk**
- ½ **cup miniature semisweet chocolate chips**
- ½ **cup chopped walnuts**
- 1½ **pounds dark chocolate candy coating, coarsely chopped**

1. In a large bowl, cream the butter and brown sugar until light and fluffy. Beat in vanilla. Gradually add flour, alternately with milk, beating well after each addition. Stir in chocolate chips and walnuts.

2. Shape into 1-in. balls; place on waxed paper-lined baking sheets. Loosely cover and refrigerate for 1-2 hours or until firm.

3. In a microwave, melt candy coating; stir until smooth. Dip balls in coating; allow excess to drip off. Place on waxed paper-lined baking sheets. Refrigerate until firm, about 15 minutes. If desired, remelt remaining candy coating and drizzle over candies. Store in the refrigerator.

STRAWBERRY CHOCOLATE TRUFFLES

Decadent truffles showcase a fun combination of strawberries and chocolate. I often double the recipe so I can give the extras to neighbors.

—PAT HABIGER SPEARVILLE, KS

PREP: 15 MIN. + CHILLING
MAKES: 3½ DOZEN

- 4 **milk chocolate candy bars (7 ounces each), halved**
- 1 **cup heavy whipping cream**
- ¼ **cup strawberry spreadable fruit**
- 1½ **teaspoons vanilla extract**
- 1¼ **cups chopped almonds, toasted**

1. Place chocolate in a food processor; cover and process until chopped. In a small saucepan, bring cream just to a boil. Pour over chocolate; cover and process until smooth. Stir in spreadable fruit and the vanilla until combined. Transfer to a small bowl; cool to room temperature, stirring occasionally. Refrigerate until firm, about 3 hours.

2. Shape into 1-in. balls. Roll in almonds.

TO MAKE AHEAD *These truffles can be made up to a week before serving. Keep refrigerated in an airtight container.*

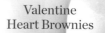
Valentine
Heart Brownies

Cookies,
Bars & More

VALENTINE HEART BROWNIES

Steal hearts this Valentine's Day (or any day!) with brownies that have cute frosting centers. They're simply irresistible.

—TASTE OF HOME TEST KITCHEN

PREP: 35 MIN.
BAKE: 20 MIN. + COOLING
MAKES: 15 SERVINGS

- 1 **package fudge brownie mix (13x9-inch pan size)**
- ¼ **teaspoon mint extract**
- ½ **cup butter, softened**
- 1½ **cups confectioners' sugar**
- ¼ **teaspoon vanilla extract**
  Red paste food coloring, optional
- ¼ **cup baking cocoa**

1. Prepare brownie mix according to package directions, adding mint extract to batter. Transfer to a greased 13x9-in. baking pan. Bake at 350° for 20-25 minutes or until a toothpick inserted near the center comes out clean. Cool completely on a wire rack.
2. Meanwhile, in a small bowl, cream the butter, confectioners' sugar, vanilla and food coloring if desired until light and fluffy. Place in a heavy-duty resealable plastic bag; cut a small hole in a corner of bag. Set aside.
3. Line a baking sheet with parchment paper. Dust with cocoa; set aside. Cut brownies into 15 rectangles. Using a 1½-in. heart-shaped cookie cutter, cut out a heart from the center of each brownie. Reserve cutout centers for another use. Place brownies on prepared baking sheet. Pipe frosting into centers of brownies.

SUGAR-CONE CHOCOLATE CHIP COOKIES

If I could make a batch of cookies a day, I'd be in baking heaven. I made these for my boys when they were growing up, and now I treat my grandkids, too.

—PAULA MARCHESI LENHARTSVILLE, PA

PREP: 25 MIN. • **BAKE:** 10 MIN./BATCH
MAKES: 6 DOZEN

- 1 **cup butter, softened**
- ¾ **cup sugar**
- ¾ **cup packed brown sugar**
- 2 **large eggs**
- 3 **teaspoons vanilla extract**
- 2¼ **cups all-purpose flour**
- 1 **teaspoon baking soda**
- ½ **teaspoon salt**
- 2 **cups milk chocolate chips**
- 2 **cups coarsely crushed ice cream sugar cones (about 16)**
- 1 **cup sprinkles**

1. Preheat oven to 375°. In a large bowl, cream butter and sugars until light and fluffy. Beat in the eggs and vanilla. In another bowl, whisk flour, baking soda and salt; gradually beat into creamed mixture. Stir in chocolate chips, crushed sugar cones and sprinkles.
2. Drop by tablespoonfuls 2 in. apart onto ungreased baking sheets. Bake 8-10 minutes or until golden brown. Remove from pans to wire racks to cool.

TURTLE COOKIE CUPS

The gooey caramel pairs wonderfully with crunchy pecans. For a twist, use white chocolate chips in the cups and drizzle with white chocolate.

—HEATHER KING FROSTBURG, MD

PREP: 35 MIN. + STANDING
BAKE: 10 MIN./BATCH + COOLING
MAKES: 4 DOZEN

- 1 **cup butter, softened**
- 1 **cup packed brown sugar**
- ½ **cup sugar**
- 2 **large eggs**
- 1 **teaspoon vanilla extract**
- 2½ **cups all-purpose flour**
- 1 **teaspoon baking soda**
- ½ **teaspoon salt**
- 1¼ **cups semisweet chocolate chips, divided**
- ½ **cup chopped pecans**
- 1 **cup Kraft caramel bits**
- 3 **tablespoons heavy whipping cream**
- 48 **pecan halves (about ¾ cup)**

1. Preheat oven to 375°. In a large bowl, cream butter and sugars until light and fluffy. Beat in eggs and vanilla. In another bowl, whisk flour, baking soda and salt; gradually beat into creamed mixture.

2. Shape dough into 1-in. balls; place in greased mini muffin cups. Press evenly onto bottoms and up the sides of cups. Bake 9-11 minutes or until edges are golden brown. With the back of measuring teaspoon, make an indentation in each cup. Immediately sprinkle with ¾ cup chocolate chips and chopped pecans. Cool in pans 10 minutes. Remove to wire racks to cool.

3. Meanwhile, in a small saucepan, melt caramel bits with cream; stir until smooth. Spoon into cups. Top each with a pecan half. In a microwave, melt remaining chocolate chips; stir until smooth. Drizzle over pecans. Let stand until set.

CHOCOLATE-COVERED MARSHMALLOW COOKIES

I've always liked to bake, and this cookie recipe was always a favorite of my eight children. Now, my 11 grandchildren also love it just as much.

—MARY MARGARET LAKE INDEPENDENCE, IA

PREP: 20 MIN. • **BAKE:** 10 MIN. + COOLING
MAKES: 3 DOZEN

- 1¾ cups sifted cake flour
- ½ cup baking cocoa
- ½ teaspoon salt
- ½ teaspoon baking soda
- ½ cup shortening
- 1 cup sugar
- 1 large egg
- 1 teaspoon vanilla extract
- ¼ cup milk
- 18 large marshmallows, halved

FROSTING

- 2 cups confectioners' sugar
- 5 tablespoons baking cocoa
- ⅛ teaspoon salt
- 3 tablespoons butter, softened
- 4 to 5 tablespoons half-and-half cream
- 36 pecan halves

1. Sift together flour, cocoa, salt and soda; set aside. In a bowl, cream shortening and sugar until light and fluffy; add the egg, vanilla and milk. Gradually add the dry ingredients and mix well.

2. Drop by heaping teaspoonfuls about 2 in. apart onto greased baking sheets. Bake at 350° for 8 minutes. Do not overbake. Remove cookies from the oven and top each with a marshmallow half. Return to oven for 2 minutes. Remove cookies to wire racks to cool.

3. Meanwhile, beat all frosting ingredients together. Spread the frosting on each cookie and top with a pecan half.

SACHER BARS

Is your mouth watering yet? This rich take on a Viennese classic using apricot preserves and chocolate left our tasters almost speechless!

—LORRAINE CALAND SHUNIAH, ON

PREP: 30 MIN. • **BAKE:** 15 MIN. + COOLING
MAKES: 6¼ DOZEN

- ¾ cup butter, cubed
- 3 ounces unsweetened chocolate, chopped
- 3 large eggs
- 1½ cups sugar
- 1½ teaspoons vanilla extract
- 1¼ cups all-purpose flour
- ¾ cup apricot preserves
- 2 ounces semisweet chocolate, chopped

1. Preheat oven to 325°. Line a greased 15x10x1-in. baking pan with waxed paper. Grease and flour the paper; set aside. In a microwave, melt butter and unsweetened chocolate; stir until smooth. In a large bowl, beat eggs and sugar. Stir in vanilla and chocolate mixture. Gradually add flour.

2. Transfer to prepared pan. Bake 15-20 minutes or until a toothpick inserted near the center comes out clean (do not overbake). Cool cake for 10 minutes before removing from pan to a wire rack to cool completely.

3. In a microwave, heat preserves until melted. Cut cake into four 7½x5-in. rectangles. Spread half of the preserves over two rectangles. Top each with the remaining cake and spread with the remaining preserves. Cut into bars.

4. In a microwave, melt semisweet chocolate; stir until smooth. Drizzle over bars. Let stand until set. Store in an airtight container in the refrigerator.

SMALL BATCH BROWNIES

Here's the perfect chocolaty treat for a small crowd. For a pretty accent, dust the tops with confectioners' sugar.

—TASTE OF HOME TEST KITCHEN

PREP: 15 MIN. • **BAKE:** 15 MIN. + COOLING
MAKES: 6 SERVINGS

- 2 **tablespoons butter**
- ½ **ounce unsweetened chocolate**
- 1 **large egg**
- ¼ **teaspoon vanilla extract**
- ⅔ **cup sugar**
- ⅓ **cup all-purpose flour**
- ¼ **cup baking cocoa**
- ¼ **teaspoon salt**
- ¼ **teaspoon confectioners' sugar, optional**

1. In a microwave, melt butter and chocolate; stir until smooth. Cool slightly.
2. In a small bowl, whisk egg and vanilla; gradually whisk in sugar. Stir in chocolate mixture. Combine the flour, cocoa and salt; gradually add to the chocolate mixture.
3. Transfer to a 9x5-in. loaf pan coated with cooking spray. Bake at 350° for 12-16 minutes or until a toothpick inserted near the center comes out clean. Cool on a wire rack. Cut into bars. Dust with confectioners' sugar if desired.

CHERRY KISS COOKIES

PREP: 20 MIN.
BAKE: 10 MIN./BATCH + COOLING
MAKES: 4½ DOZEN

- 1 **cup butter, softened**
- 1 **cup confectioners' sugar**
- ½ **teaspoon salt**
- 2 **teaspoons maraschino cherry juice**
- ½ **teaspoon almond extract**
- 6 **drops red food coloring, optional**
- 2¼ **cups all-purpose flour**
- ½ **cup chopped maraschino cherries**
- 54 **milk chocolate kisses, unwrapped**

1. Preheat oven to 350°. In a large bowl, beat butter, confectioners' sugar and salt until blended. Beat in the cherry juice, extract and, if desired, food coloring. Gradually beat in flour. Stir in cherries.
2. Shape dough into 1-in. balls. Place 1 in. apart on greased baking sheets.
3. Bake 8-10 minutes or until bottoms are light brown. Immediately press a chocolate kiss into center of each cookie (cookie will crack around edges). Cool on pans for 2 minutes. Remove to wire racks to cool.

Chocolate-covered-cherry lovers, get ready for this delicious dessert. This playful variation on thumbprint cookies will be your new favorite special treat.

—JOY YURK GRAFTON, WI

BLACK FOREST ICEBOX COOKIES

You'll want to keep extra batches of these tasty cookies for when company drops by. The rich chocolate wafers and sweet-tart filling go perfectly together.

—*TASTE OF HOME* TEST KITCHEN

PREP: 20 MIN. + CHILLING
MAKES: 20 COOKIES

- 3 **tablespoons sugar**
- 4 **teaspoons cornstarch**
  Pinch salt
- ¾ **cup fresh or frozen pitted tart cherries, thawed and coarsely chopped**
- ¾ **cup cherry juice blend**
- 1½ **teaspoons lemon juice**
- 1 **to 2 drops red food coloring, optional**
- ½ **cup mascarpone cheese**
- 1 **tablespoon confectioners' sugar**
- 1 **teaspoon cherry brandy**
- 1 **package (9 ounces) chocolate wafers**
- ½ **cup semisweet chocolate chips**
- ¼ **cup heavy whipping cream**

1. In a small saucepan, combine the sugar, cornstarch and salt. Add the cherries, juice blend and lemon juice. Bring to a boil; cook and stir for 2 minutes or until thickened. Remove from the heat and stir in food coloring if desired. Cool to room temperature.

2. In a small bowl, combine the mascarpone cheese, confectioners' sugar and brandy. Spread about 1 teaspoon cheese mixture onto 20 wafers; top with 2 teaspoons cherry mixture and remaining wafers. Place on a waxed paper-lined baking pan. Place chocolate chips in a small bowl. In a small saucepan, bring cream just to a boil. Pour over chips; whisk until smooth. Drizzle over cookies. Cover and refrigerate cookies for up to 4 hours before serving.

BUTTERFINGER COOKIE BARS

My boys went through a phase where they really loved Butterfingers. We made Butterfinger shakes, muffins, cookies and tested different bars; this one was voted the best of the bunch. Make sure you have an extra candy bar on hand because it's hard to resist a nibble or two while you're chopping.
—**BARBARA LEIGHTY** SIMI VALLEY, CA

PREP: 20 MIN. • **BAKE:** 25 MIN. + COOLING
MAKES: 3 DOZEN

- 1 **package dark chocolate cake mix (regular size)**
- 1 **cup all-purpose flour**
- 1 **package (3.9 ounces) instant chocolate pudding mix**
- 1 **tablespoon baking cocoa**
- ½ **cup 2% milk**
- ⅓ **cup canola oil**
- ⅓ **cup butter, melted**
- 2 **large eggs, divided use**
- 6 **Butterfinger candy bars (2.1 ounces each), divided**
- 1½ **cups chunky peanut butter**
- 1 **teaspoon vanilla extract**
- 1½ **cups semisweet chocolate chips, divided**

1. Preheat oven to 350°. In a large bowl, combine the cake mix, flour, pudding mix and cocoa. In another bowl, whisk milk, oil, butter and 1 egg until blended. Add to dry ingredients; stir just until moistened. Press half of the mixture into a greased 15x10x1-in. baking pan. Bake 10 minutes.

2. Meanwhile, chop two candy bars. Stir peanut butter, vanilla and remaining egg into remaining cake mix mixture. Fold in chopped bars and 1 cup chocolate chips.

3. Chop three additional candy bars; sprinkle over warm crust and press down gently. Cover with cake mix mixture; press down firmly with a metal spatula. Crush remaining candy bar; sprinkle crushed bar and the remaining chocolate chips over top.

4. Bake 25-30 minutes or until a toothpick inserted into center comes out clean. Cool on a wire rack. Cut into bars. Store in an airtight container.

BAKING MORSELS

MOCHA MACAROON COOKIES

Here's an updated version of the classic macaroon. With chocolate, coffee and cinnamon, it tastes like a specialty from a barista. Your java-drinking friends will love it!

—**JEANNE HOLT** MENDOTA HEIGHTS, MN

PREP: 20 MIN.
BAKE: 10 MIN./BATCH + COOLING
MAKES: 4 DOZEN

- 2 **teaspoons instant coffee granules**
- 2 **teaspoons hot water**
- 1 **can (14 ounces) sweetened condensed milk**
- 2 **ounces unsweetened chocolate, melted**
- 1 **teaspoon vanilla extract**
- ¼ **teaspoon ground cinnamon**
- ⅛ **teaspoon salt**
- 1 **package (14 ounces) flaked coconut**
- ⅔ **cup white baking chips, melted**
  Plain or chocolate-covered coffee beans

1. Preheat oven to 350°. In a large bowl, dissolve coffee granules in hot water. Stir in condensed milk, melted chocolate, vanilla, cinnamon and salt until blended. Stir in coconut. Drop mixture by rounded teaspoonfuls 2 in. apart onto parchment paper-lined baking sheets.

2. Bake 10-12 minutes or until set. Cool on pans 1 minute. Remove from pans to wire racks to cool completely.

3. Drizzle cookies with melted baking chips. Top with coffee beans, attaching with melted chips if necessary.

SUPER SPUD BROWNIES

I came across the recipe for these tender, cake-like brownies in my mom's old cookbook. Mashed potatoes may seem like an unusual ingredient, but this recipe won first place at a local festival.

—**MARLENE GERER** DENTON, MT

PREP: 15 MIN. • **BAKE:** 25 MIN.
MAKES: 16 SERVINGS

- ¾ **cup mashed potatoes**
- ½ **cup sugar**
- ½ **cup packed brown sugar**
- ½ **cup canola oil**
- 2 **large eggs, lightly beaten**
- 1 **teaspoon vanilla extract**
- ½ **cup all-purpose flour**
- ⅓ **cup cocoa powder**
- ½ **teaspoon baking powder**
- ⅛ **teaspoon salt**
- ½ **cup chopped pecans, optional**
  Confectioners' sugar

1. In a large bowl, combine the mashed potatoes, sugars, oil, eggs and vanilla. Combine the flour, cocoa, baking powder and salt; gradually add to potato mixture. Fold in pecans if desired. Transfer to a greased 9-in. square baking pan.

2. Bake at 350° for 23-27 minutes or until a toothpick inserted near the center comes out clean. Cool on a wire rack. Dust with confectioners' sugar. Cut into bars.

HAWAIIAN JOY BARS

I get rave reviews when I bring these to work or to church. It's like a trip to the islands with the nuts and hint of rum!

—JENNIFER NECKERMANN
WENTZVILLE, MO

PREP: 20 MIN. • **BAKE:** 35 MIN. + COOLING
MAKES: 2 DOZEN

- 1 cup butter, melted
- 2 cups packed brown sugar
- 2 large eggs, lightly beaten
- ⅓ cup rum
- 3 teaspoons vanilla extract
- 2 cups all-purpose flour
- 2 teaspoons baking powder
- 1 teaspoon baking soda
- ½ teaspoon salt
- 2¼ cups semisweet chocolate chips, divided
- 1 package (10 to 12 ounces) white baking chips
- 1½ cups flaked coconut
- 1½ cups macadamia nuts, chopped
- 1 teaspoon shortening
- 1 ounce white candy coating, melted

1. In a large bowl, stir the butter, brown sugar, eggs, rum and vanilla until well blended. Combine the flour, baking powder, baking soda and salt; gradually add to butter mixture. Stir in 2 cups chocolate chips, white chips, coconut and nuts.

2. Pour into a greased 13x9-in. baking pan. Bake at 350° for 35-40 minutes or until golden brown. Cool on a wire rack.

3. In a microwave, melt shortening with the remaining chocolate chips; drizzle over bars. Drizzle candy coating over the bars. Store in an airtight container.

FUDGY BROWNIES WITH PEANUT BUTTER PUDDING FROSTING

PREP: 20 MIN. • **BAKE:** 25 MIN. + CHILLING
MAKES: 2½ DOZEN

- 1 package fudge brownie mix (13x9-inch pan size)
- 1½ cups confectioners' sugar
- ½ cup butter, softened
- 2 to 3 tablespoons peanut butter
- 2 tablespoons cold 2% milk
- 4½ teaspoons instant vanilla pudding mix
- 1 can (16 ounces) chocolate fudge frosting

1. Prepare and bake the brownies according to package directions. Cool on a wire rack.

2. Meanwhile, in a small bowl, beat the confectioners' sugar, butter, peanut butter, milk and pudding mix until smooth. Spread over the brownies. Refrigerate for 30 minutes or until firm. Frost with chocolate fudge frosting just before cutting.

Rich brownies are topped with a peanut butter pudding frosting, making this a recipe the whole family will love. These are perfect for a potluck, bake sale or yummy after-dinner treat.

—AMY CROOK SYRACUSE, UT

Chocolate-Mint
Cookie Cups

CHOCOLATE-MINT COOKIE CUPS

Peppermint adds a fresh bite to these pretty chocolate cookies. They're my holiday party go-to. If you don't have mini muffin pans, use disposable foil baking cups.

—PAM CORRELL BROCKPORT, PA

PREP: 45 MIN. + CHILLING • **BAKE:** 10 MIN./BATCH
MAKES: 4 DOZEN

- ½ **cup butter, softened**
- 1 **cup sugar**
- 1 **large egg**
- 1 **teaspoon peppermint extract**
- 1½ **cups all-purpose flour**
- ½ **cup baking cocoa**
- ¼ **teaspoon baking soda**
- ¼ **teaspoon baking powder**
- ¼ **teaspoon salt**

TOPPING

- 1 **cup (6 ounces) semisweet chocolate chips**
- ½ **cup heavy whipping cream**
- ¼ **cup white baking chips**
  Green paste food coloring, optional

1. Preheat oven to 350°. In a large bowl, cream butter and sugar until light and fluffy. Beat in egg and extract. Combine flour, cocoa, baking soda, baking powder and salt; gradually add to creamed mixture and mix well.

2. Shape into 1-in. balls; place in paper-lined miniature muffin cups. Bake 8-10 minutes or until set. Remove to wire racks. Cool completely.

3. Place chocolate chips in a small bowl. In a small saucepan, bring cream just to a boil. Pour over chocolate; whisk until smooth. Cool to room temperature, stirring occasionally. Refrigerate until ganache reaches a piping consistency, about 20 minutes. Pipe over the cookies.

4. In a microwave-safe bowl, melt white baking chips at 50% power for 1 minute; stir until smooth. If desired, tint with green food coloring. Pipe over tops.

BAKING MORSELS

CARAMEL-CASHEW DARK CHOCOLATE CHIPPERS

The flavor of this treat is wonderful. My family likes to sandwich a scoop of vanilla ice cream between two cookies. It makes a special treat.
—**PAM IVBULS** OMAHA, NE

PREP: 25 MIN. • **BAKE:** 15 MIN./BATCH
MAKES: 3 DOZEN

- 4 **cups salted cashews**
- 1 **cup sugar**
- 1 **cup packed brown sugar**
- 1 **cup butter, softened**
- 1 **can (13.4 ounces) dulce de leche**
- 4 **large eggs**
- ⅓ **cup buttermilk**
- 2 **teaspoons vanilla extract**
- 5 **cups biscuit/baking mix**
- 2 **packages (12 ounces each) dark chocolate chips**
  Additional sugar

1. Place cashews and sugars in a food processor; cover and process until nuts are finely chopped.

2. In a large bowl, beat butter and dulce de leche until blended. Beat in the eggs, buttermilk and vanilla. Combine baking mix and cashew mixture; gradually add to butter mixture and mix well. Stir in chocolate chips (dough will be sticky).

3. Drop dough by ¼ cupfuls 4 in. apart onto parchment paper-lined baking sheets. Coat bottom of a glass with cooking spray, then dip into additional sugar. Flatten cookies with prepared glass to 2½-in. circles, redipping in sugar as needed.

4. Bake at 325° for 15-18 minutes or until edges begin to brown. Cool for 3 minutes before removing from pans to wire racks.

NOTE *This recipe was tested with Nestle La Lechera dulce de leche; look for it in the international foods section. If using Eagle Brand dulce de leche (caramel-flavored sauce), thicken according to the package directions before using.*

BAKING MORSELS

JUMBO BROWNIE COOKIES

Bring these deeply fudgy cookies to a party and you're sure to make a friend. A little espresso powder in the dough makes them even more over-the-top.
—**REBECCA CABABA** LAS VEGAS, NV

PREP: 20 MIN. • **BAKE:** 15 MIN./BATCH
MAKES: ABOUT 1½ DOZEN

- 2⅔ **cups (16 ounces) 60% cacao bittersweet chocolate baking chips**
- ½ **cup unsalted butter, cubed**
- 4 **large eggs**
- 1½ **cups sugar**
- 4 **teaspoons vanilla extract**
- 2 **teaspoons instant espresso powder, optional**
- ⅔ **cup all-purpose flour**
- ½ **teaspoon baking powder**
- ¼ **teaspoon salt**
- 1 **package (11½ ounces) semisweet chocolate chunks**

1. Preheat oven to 350°. In a large saucepan, melt chocolate chips and butter over low heat, stirring until smooth. Remove from the heat; cool until mixture is warm.

2. In a small bowl, whisk the eggs, sugar, vanilla and, if desired, espresso powder until blended. Whisk into the chocolate mixture. In another bowl, mix the flour, baking powder and salt; add to chocolate mixture, mixing well. Fold in chocolate chunks; let stand 10 minutes or until mixture thickens slightly.

3. Drop by ¼ cupfuls 3 in. apart onto parchment paper-lined baking sheets. Bake 12-14 minutes or until set. Cool on pans 1-2 minutes. Remove to wire racks to cool.

NOTE *This recipe was tested with Ghirardelli 60% Cacao Bittersweet Chocolate Baking Chips; results may vary when using a different product.*

HOT CHOCOLATE PEPPERMINT COOKIES

This is a variation of the cookies my mother made when I was growing up, and now my teenage daughter and I bake them together. They're always a huge hit!
—**LARRY PIKLOR** JOHNSBURG, IL

PREP: 30 MIN.
BAKE: 10 MIN./BATCH + COOLING
MAKES: 3½ DOZEN

- 1 **cup butter, softened**
- 1 **cup sugar**
- 1 **large egg**
- 1 **teaspoon peppermint extract**
- 2⅓ **cups all-purpose flour**
- ⅓ **cup baking cocoa**
- 1 **teaspoon salt**
- 1 **teaspoon baking soda**
- 1 **package (11½ ounces) milk chocolate chips**
- 1 **cup marshmallow creme**
- 1 **cup finely crushed peppermint candies**

1. Cream butter and sugar in a large bowl until light and fluffy. Beat in egg and extract. Combine the flour, cocoa, salt and baking soda; gradually add to creamed mixture and mix well.

2. Drop by tablespoonfuls 2 in. apart onto greased baking sheets. Bake at 375° for 10-12 minutes or until tops are cracked. Remove to wire racks to cool completely.

3. Melt the chocolate chips in a microwave; stir until smooth. Drop a teaspoonful of marshmallow creme into the center of each cookie. Dip half of each cookie into melted chocolate; allow excess to drip off. Immediately sprinkle with candies. Place on waxed paper and let stand until set. Store in an airtight container.

TO MAKE AHEAD *Bake and cool cookies as directed. Freeze for up to 1 month. Several hours before serving, proceed with finishing cookies as directed.*

MILLION DOLLAR PECAN BARS

Invest 15 minutes of your time and enjoy a big payoff when you pull these rich bars of golden layered goodness from your own oven.
—**LAURA DAVIS** RUSK, TX

PREP: 15 MIN. • **BAKE:** 20 MIN.
MAKES: 2 DOZEN

¾ cup butter, softened
¾ cup packed brown sugar
2 large eggs
2 teaspoons vanilla extract
1 package butter pecan cake mix
(regular size)
2½ cups quick-cooking oats
FILLING
1 can (14 ounces) sweetened
condensed milk
2 cups milk chocolate chips
1 cup butterscotch chips
1 tablespoon butter
1 teaspoon vanilla extract
1½ cups chopped pecans

1. In a large bowl, cream butter and brown sugar until light and fluffy. Add eggs, one at a time, beating well after each addition. Beat in vanilla. Add cake mix just until blended. Stir in the oats. Press 3 cups of mixture onto bottom of a greased 13x9-in. baking pan.
2. In a large microwave-safe bowl, combine milk and chips. Microwave, uncovered, on high for 2 minutes; stir. Cook 1-2½ minutes longer or until chips are melted, stirring every 30 seconds. Stir in butter and vanilla until melted. Stir in pecans. Spread over crust.
3. Crumble remaining oat mixture; sprinkle over the top. Bake at 350° for 20-25 minutes or until the topping is golden brown. Cool on a wire rack. Cut into bars.

CRANBERRY-PORT FUDGE BROWNIES

These fudgy brownies are my friend Krysta's favorite! The port wine adds a sophisticated flavor to this decadent dessert.
—**KELLY HEFT** SOMERSVILLE, MA

PREP: 25 MIN. • **BAKE:** 30 MIN. + COOLING
MAKES: 16 SERVINGS

4 ounces unsweetened chocolate,
chopped
½ cup butter, cubed
1½ cups sugar
½ teaspoon vanilla extract
2 large eggs
¾ cup all-purpose flour
¼ teaspoon salt
½ cup dried cranberries
½ cup tawny port wine

1. In a small saucepan, melt chocolate and butter; stir until smooth. Remove from the heat; stir in sugar and vanilla. Add eggs, one at a time, stirring well after each addition. Stir in flour and salt just until blended. In another small saucepan, combine cranberries and wine. Bring to a boil over medium heat; cook until liquid is reduced to a thin, syrupy consistency (about 3 minutes). Stir into batter.
2. Transfer to a greased 9-in. square baking pan. Bake at 325° for 30-35 minutes or until a toothpick inserted near the center comes out clean (do not overbake). Cool on a wire rack.

BAKING MORSELS

_____
_____
_____
_____
_____
_____
_____
_____
_____
_____
_____
_____
_____
_____
_____
_____
_____
_____
_____
_____
_____
_____
_____
_____
_____
_____
_____
_____
_____
_____
_____
_____
_____
_____
_____
_____
_____

RASPBERRY & CHOCOLATE SHORTBREAD BARS

When I was a child, I decided that chocolate and raspberries were a combination made in heaven, and that any treat made with these two delicious ingredients would be at the top of my holiday list. Any seedless jam or preserves may be used, but raspberry is our favorite.

—LILY JULOW LAWRENCEVILLE, GA

PREP: 25 MIN. • **BAKE:** 30 MIN. + COOLING
MAKES: 2 DOZEN

- 1 **cup unsalted butter, softened**
- 1 **cup sugar**
- 2 **large egg yolks**
- ½ **teaspoon vanilla extract**
- 2 **cups all-purpose flour**
- 1 **teaspoon baking powder**
- ¼ **teaspoon salt**
- 1 **jar (10 ounces) seedless raspberry spreadable fruit**
- 4 **ounces bittersweet chocolate, finely chopped**
- ⅓ **cup heavy whipping cream**

1. Preheat oven to 350°. In a large bowl, cream butter and sugar until light and fluffy. Beat in egg yolks and vanilla. In a small bowl, mix flour, baking powder and salt; gradually add to the creamed mixture, mixing well.

2. Press half of the dough onto bottom of a greased 11x7-in. baking dish. Top with the spreadable fruit. Crumble remaining dough over fruit. Bake on lowest oven rack for 30-40 minutes or until golden brown. Cool completely on a wire rack.

3. Place chocolate in a small bowl. In a small saucepan, bring cream just to a boil. Pour over chocolate; stir with a whisk until smooth. Drizzle over top of shortbread; let stand until set. Cut into bars.

Raspberry & Chocolate
Shortbread Bars

CHERRY-CHOCOLATE OATMEAL COOKIES

My kids love making these home-style cookies. They're so wonderful when warm.
—**JAYE BEELER** GRAND RAPIDS, MI

PREP: 25 MIN. • **BAKE:** 10 MIN./BATCH
MAKES: 6 DOZEN

- 1 **cup butter, softened**
- 1½ **cups packed brown sugar**
- 2 **large eggs**
- 1 **teaspoon vanilla extract**
- 1½ **cups all-purpose flour**
- 1 **teaspoon ground cinnamon**
- ½ **teaspoon baking powder**
- ½ **teaspoon baking soda**
- ½ **teaspoon salt**
- 2 **cups old-fashioned oats**
- 1 **cup dried tart cherries**
- 1 **cup dark chocolate chips**

1. Preheat oven to 350°. In a large bowl, cream butter and brown sugar until light and fluffy. Beat in eggs and vanilla. In another bowl, whisk flour, cinnamon, baking powder, baking soda and salt; gradually beat into creamed mixture. Stir in oats, cherries and chocolate chips.

2. Drop by tablespoonfuls 2 in. apart onto ungreased baking sheets. Bake 9-11 minutes or until edges are golden brown. Cool on pans 1 minute. Remove to wire racks to cool.

CHOCOLATE-PUMPKIN CHEESECAKE BARS

I created these bars by taking my well loved cheesecake brownie recipe, and then kicking it up with pumpkin and spices. They always disappear fast, so consider making two pans.

—JUDY CASTRANOVA NEW BERN, NC

PREP: 30 MIN. • **BAKE:** 20 MIN.
MAKES: 2 DOZEN

- ⅓ **cup butter, cubed**
- 1½ **ounces unsweetened chocolate, coarsely chopped**
- 1 **tablespoon instant coffee granules**
- ½ **cup boiling water**
- 1 **cup canned pumpkin**
- 2 **large eggs, lightly beaten**
- 2 **cups all-purpose flour**
- 1½ **cups sugar**
- ¾ **teaspoon baking soda**
- ½ **teaspoon salt**

CHEESECAKE BATTER
- 1 **package (8 ounces) reduced-fat cream cheese**
- ½ **cup canned pumpkin**
- ¼ **cup sugar**
- 1 **teaspoon vanilla extract**
- ¾ **teaspoon ground cinnamon**
- ¾ **teaspoon ground ginger**
- ⅛ **teaspoon ground cloves**
- 1 **large egg, lightly beaten**
- 1 **cup (6 ounces) semisweet chocolate chips**

1. In a microwave, melt the butter and chocolate; stir until smooth. Cool slightly.

2. In a large bowl, dissolve coffee in water. Stir in the pumpkin, eggs and chocolate mixture. Combine the flour, sugar, baking soda and salt; gradually add to chocolate mixture. Transfer to a 15x10x1-in. baking pan coated with cooking spray.

3. For cheesecake batter, in a small bowl, beat cream cheese and pumpkin until smooth. Beat in the sugar, vanilla and spices. Add egg; beat on low speed just until combined. Spoon over the chocolate batter. Cut through batter with a knife to swirl the cheesecake portion. Sprinkle with chocolate chips.

4. Bake at 350° for 20-25 minutes or until a toothpick inserted near the center comes out with moist crumbs (do not overbake). Cool on a wire rack. Cut into bars. Refrigerate leftovers.

BAKING MORSELS

MINT-MALLOW SANDWICH COOKIES

My lightened-up version of whoopie pies with a peppermint twist is popular with the kids, especially around the holidays.

—DION FRISCHER ANN ARBOR, MI

PREP: 30 MIN. • **BAKE:** 10 MIN./BATCH
MAKES: 2 DOZEN

- ⅓ **cup butter, softened**
- 1¼ **cups sugar**
- 1 **large egg white**
- 1 **teaspoon vanilla extract**
- 1 **cup all-purpose flour**
- ⅓ **cup baking cocoa**
- ¼ **teaspoon baking soda**

FILLING

- ⅓ **cup marshmallow creme**
- ⅛ **teaspoon peppermint extract**
- 1 **drop red food coloring, optional**

1. In a large bowl, beat butter and sugar until crumbly, about 2 minutes. Beat in the egg white and vanilla. Combine the flour, cocoa and baking soda; gradually add to sugar mixture and mix well.

2. Shape into ¾-in. balls; place 2 in. apart on baking sheets coated with cooking spray. Bake at 350° for 7-9 minutes or until set. Remove to wire racks to cool completely.

3. In a small bowl, combine the marshmallow creme, extract and food coloring if desired. Spread on the bottoms of half of the cookies; top with remaining cookies. Store in an airtight container.

CHOCOLATY S'MORES BARS

PREP: 15 MIN. + COOLING
MAKES: 1½ DOZEN

- ¼ **cup butter, cubed**
- 1 **package (10 ounces) large marshmallows**
- 1 **package (12 ounces) Golden Grahams**
- ⅓ **cup milk chocolate chips, melted**

1. In a large saucepan, melt butter over low heat. Add marshmallows; cook and stir until blended. Remove from heat. Stir in cereal until coated.

2. Using a buttered spatula, press evenly into a greased 13x9-in. pan. Drizzle with melted chocolate chips. Cool completely. Cut into bars. Store in an airtight container.

One night, my husband had some friends over to play poker and he asked for these s'mores bars. They polished off the pan! I shared the recipe so his friends could make them at home, too.

—REBECCA SHIPP BEEBE, AR

ANGELA'S XOXO SHORTBREAD BROWNIES

Everyone loves brownies! This one has a buttery crust with a sweet finish, thanks to the touch of candy on top.

—ANGELA KAMAKANA BAPTISTA HILO, HI

PREP: 15 MIN. • **BAKE:** 40 MIN. + COOLING
MAKES: 16 SERVINGS

- 2 **cups all-purpose flour**
- ½ **cup sugar**
- 1 **cup cold butter, cubed**
- 1 **package fudge brownie mix (13x9-inch pan size)**
- 8 **striped chocolate kisses, unwrapped**
- 8 **milk chocolate kisses, unwrapped**
- ½ **cup M&M's Minis**

1. In a large bowl, mix flour and sugar; cut in butter until crumbly. Press onto the bottom of a greased 13x9-in. baking pan. Bake at 350° for 17-20 minutes or until lightly browned. Cool on a wire rack.

2. Prepare brownie mix batter according to package directions; spread over crust. Bake 23-28 minutes longer or until a toothpick inserted into center comes out clean (do not overbake). Immediately top with kisses and M&M's, spacing evenly and pressing down lightly to adhere. Cool in pan on a wire rack.

CAFE MOCHA COOKIES

These coffee cookies are crispy outside, but soft in the middle. So good!

—**ANGELA SPENGLER** TAMPA, FL

PREP: 20 MIN. • **BAKE:** 10 MIN./BATCH
MAKES: ABOUT 3 DOZEN

- 6 **tablespoons butter, softened**
- ⅓ **cup shortening**
- ½ **cup packed brown sugar**
- ⅓ **cup sugar**
- 1 **large egg**
- 2 **tablespoons hot caramel ice cream topping**
- 1 **teaspoon vanilla extract**
- 1½ **cups all-purpose flour**
- 4 **teaspoons dark roast instant coffee granules**
- ½ **teaspoon baking soda**
- ½ **teaspoon salt**
- 1½ **cups (9 ounces) dark chocolate chips**

1. Preheat oven to 350°. In a large bowl, cream the butter, shortening and sugars until light and fluffy. Beat in the egg, ice cream topping and vanilla. In another bowl, whisk the flour, coffee granules, baking soda and salt; gradually beat into creamed mixture. Fold in chocolate chips.

2. Drop the dough by rounded tablespoonfuls 2 in. apart onto ungreased baking sheets. Bake 8-10 minutes or until set. Cool on pans for 2 minutes. Remove to wire racks to cool completely.

FREEZE OPTION *Drop dough by rounded tablespoonfuls onto waxed paper-lined baking sheets; freeze until firm. Transfer to resealable plastic freezer bags; return to freezer. To use, bake frozen cookies as directed, increasing the time by 1-2 minutes.*

Cafe Mocha
Cookies

SWAPPING BUTTER FOR SHORTENING

Butter can be substituted for shortening in equal amounts in cookie recipes, but it will slightly alter the cookies. Cookies made with all butter have a richer, more buttery flavor, spread more and have a darker color.

CHOCOLATE-DIPPED SPUMONI COOKIES

I mixed my favorite cookie and ice cream into one dessert. With so many flavors going on, it's hard to stop at just one cookie.

—**ERICA INGRAM** LAKEWOOD, OH

PREP: 20 MIN.
BAKE: 10 MIN./BATCH + COOLING
MAKES: ABOUT 6 DOZEN

- 1 **cup butter, softened**
- ¾ **cup sugar**
- ¾ **cup packed brown sugar**
- 2 **large eggs**
- 1 **tablespoon vanilla extract**
- 2½ **cups all-purpose flour**
- ½ **cup Dutch-processed cocoa**
- 1 **teaspoon baking soda**
- ½ **teaspoon salt**
- 1⅓ **cups finely chopped pistachios, divided**
- 1⅓ **cups finely chopped dried cherries, divided**
- 1¾ **cups semisweet chocolate chips**
- 1 **tablespoon shortening**

1. Preheat oven to 350°. In a large bowl, cream butter and sugars until light and fluffy. Beat in eggs and vanilla. In another bowl, whisk flour, cocoa, baking soda and salt; gradually beat into creamed mixture. Stir in 1 cup each pistachios and cherries.

2. Drop by tablespoonfuls 2 in. apart onto ungreased baking sheets. Bake 10-12 minutes or until set. Cool on pans 2 minutes. Remove to wire racks to cool completely.

3. In a microwave, melt chocolate chips and shortening; stir until smooth. Dip each cookie halfway into chocolate, allowing excess to drip off; sprinkle with remaining pistachios and cherries. Place on waxed paper; let stand until set.

ORANGE NANAIMO BARS

I originally created these rich bars for my co-workers. Everyone raved over the orange and chocolate combination, which sets these apart from most other bars. They're now a staple for many gatherings.
—**DEL MASON** MARTENSVILLE, SK

PREP: 40 MIN. + CHILLING
MAKES: 3 DOZEN

- ⅓ **cup butter, cubed**
- ¼ **cup sugar**
- 1 **dark chocolate candy bar (3¼ ounces), chopped**
- 1 **large egg, beaten**
- 17 **shortbread cookies, crushed**
- ½ **cup flaked coconut**
- ½ **cup finely chopped pecans**
- 1 **teaspoon grated orange peel**

FILLING
- ½ **cup butter, softened**
- 2 **tablespoons instant vanilla pudding mix**
- 2 **cups confectioners' sugar**
- 2 **tablespoons orange juice**
- 1 **teaspoon grated orange peel**
- 1 **to 2 drops orange paste food coloring, optional**

GLAZE
- 1 **dark chocolate candy bar (3¼ ounces), chopped**
- 1 **teaspoon butter**

1. In a large heavy saucepan, combine the butter, sugar and candy bar. Cook and stir over medium-low heat until melted. Whisk a small amount of hot mixture into egg. Return all to the pan, whisking constantly. Cook and stir over medium-low heat until mixture reaches 160°.

2. In a large bowl, combine the cookie crumbs, coconut, pecans and orange peel. Stir in the chocolate mixture until blended. Press into a greased 9-in. square baking pan. Refrigerate for 30 minutes or until set.

3. For filling, in a large bowl, cream butter and pudding mix. Beat in the confectioners' sugar, orange juice, peel and, if desired, food coloring. Spread over crust. For glaze, melt candy bar and butter in a microwave; stir until smooth. Spread over top. Refrigerate until set. Cut into bars.

BAKING MORSELS

Minty Chocolate
Cream Cheese Bars

MINTY CHOCOLATE CREAM CHEESE BARS

PREP: 15 MIN. • **BAKE:** 30 MIN. + COOLING
MAKES: 2 DOZEN

- 1 **package chocolate cake mix (regular size)**
- ½ **cup butter, softened**
- 1 **teaspoon almond extract**
- 1 **teaspoon vanilla extract**
- 4 **large eggs, divided use**
- 1 **package (10 ounces) Andes creme de menthe baking chips, divided**
- 1 **package (8 ounces) cream cheese, softened**
- 1⅔ **cups confectioners' sugar**

1. Preheat oven to 350°. In a large bowl, beat the cake mix, butter, extracts and 2 eggs until blended. Spread into a greased 13x9-in. baking pan. Sprinkle with ¾ cup baking chips.

2. In a small bowl, beat cream cheese and confectioners' sugar until smooth. Add the remaining eggs; beat on low speed just until blended. Pour over chocolate layer, spreading evenly; sprinkle with remaining baking chips.

3. Bake 30-35 minutes or until edges begin to brown. Cool in pan on a wire rack. Cut into bars. Refrigerate leftovers.

> I always looked forward to my grandma's decadent cream cheese bars when I was growing up. This version includes mint, which is one of my favorite flavor add-ins.
>
> **—JILL LUTZ** WOODBURY, MN

BEST OF BOTH COOKIES

Our kids ask the most for peanut butter and chocolate chip cookies, so I came up with a recipe that combines the two. The doughs swirl together to create a lovely marbled pattern in the cookie. They are so pretty on their own that there's no need for additional decorations.

—LORI KESINGER BAKER, MT

PREP: 25 MIN. + CHILLING
BAKE: 10 MIN./BATCH
MAKES: ABOUT 6½ DOZEN

- ¾ **cup creamy peanut butter**
- ½ **cup butter, softened**
- ½ **cup sugar**
- ½ **cup packed brown sugar**
- 1 **large egg**
- 1¼ **cups all-purpose flour**
- ½ **teaspoon baking powder**
- ½ **teaspoon baking soda**
- ¼ **teaspoon salt**

CHOCOLATE DOUGH
- ½ **cup butter, softened**
- ½ **cup sugar**
- ½ **cup packed brown sugar**
- 1 **large egg**
- 1 **teaspoon vanilla extract**
- 1¼ **cups all-purpose flour**
- ¼ **cup baking cocoa**
- ½ **teaspoon baking powder**
- ½ **teaspoon baking soda**
- ¼ **teaspoon salt**

1. In a large bowl, cream the peanut butter, butter and sugars until light and fluffy, about 4 minutes. Beat in egg. Combine the flour, baking powder, baking soda and salt; gradually add to creamed mixture and mix well.

2. For the chocolate dough, in another large bowl, cream butter and sugars until light and fluffy. Beat in egg and vanilla. Combine the flour, cocoa, baking powder, baking soda and salt; gradually add to creamed mixture and mix well.

3. Divide each portion in half. Knead one peanut butter and one chocolate portion together 5-10 times or until it just begins to swirl. Shape into a 10-in. log. Wrap in plastic wrap. Repeat with the remaining dough. Refrigerate for 3-4 hours or until firm.

4. Preheat oven to 350°. Unwrap dough and cut into ¼-in. slices. Place 2 in. apart on lightly greased baking sheets. Bake 6-8 minutes or until bottoms are lightly browned. Cool for 2 minutes before removing from pans to wire racks.

FREEZE OPTION *Place wrapped logs in resealable plastic freezer bag; freeze. To use, unwrap frozen logs and cut into slices. If necessary, let dough stand a few minutes at room temperature before cutting. Bake as directed.*

GRANDMA'S TANDY KAKE

My grandmother made this for all our family gatherings. Everyone loves it, and now I make it for every party we attend or host.

—**JOHN MORGAN** LEBANON, PA

PREP: 20 MIN. • **BAKE:** 20 MIN.+ CHILLING
MAKES: 24 SERVINGS

- 4 **large eggs**
- 2 **cups sugar**
- 1 **cup 2% milk**
- 1 **teaspoon vanilla extract**
- 2 **cups all-purpose flour**
- 1 **teaspoon baking powder**
- ¼ **teaspoon salt**
- 1¾ **cups creamy peanut butter**
- 5 **milk chocolate candy bars (1.55 ounces each), chopped**
- 2 **tablespoons butter**

1. Preheat oven to 350°. In a large bowl, beat eggs and sugar until thick and lemon-colored. Beat in milk and vanilla. In another bowl, combine the flour, baking powder and salt; gradually add to egg mixture and mix well.

2. Spread into a greased 15x10x1-in. baking pan. Bake 20-25 minutes or until lightly browned. Cool 15 minutes on a wire rack. Spread peanut butter over top; cool completely.

3. In a double boiler or metal bowl over simmering water, melt chocolate and butter; stir until smooth. Gently spread over peanut butter. Refrigerate 30 minutes or until firm.

EYES-WIDE-OPEN ESPRESSO COOKIES

Sometimes you just need a little pick-me-up treat. So go ahead and munch on these coffee-laced cookies!

—TASTE OF HOME TEST KITCHEN

PREP: 25 MIN. • **BAKE:** 10 MIN./BATCH
MAKES: 45 COOKIES

- ½ **cup butter, softened**
- ½ **cup sugar**
- ¼ **cup packed brown sugar**
- 1 **large egg**
- 1¼ **cups all-purpose flour**
- 6 **tablespoons baking cocoa**
- 2 **teaspoons finely ground espresso beans**
- ½ **teaspoon baking soda**
- ¼ **teaspoon salt**
- 1 **cup (6 ounces) semisweet chocolate chips**
- 45 **chocolate-covered coffee beans**

1. In a large bowl, cream the butter and sugars until light and fluffy. Beat in egg. Combine the flour, cocoa, espresso beans, baking soda and salt; gradually add to creamed mixture and mix well. Stir in chocolate chips.

2. Drop by rounded teaspoonfuls 2 in. apart onto parchment paper-lined baking sheets. Bake at 350° for 8-10 minutes or until surfaces crack. Immediately press a coffee bean into the center of each cookie. Cool for 2 minutes before removing from pans to wire racks. Store cookies in an airtight container.

CHAI CHOCOLATE CHIP SHORTBREAD

I've always loved the taste of chai tea, so I decided to try to incorporate it into one of my recipes. Everyone who samples this shortbread marvels at how delicious it tastes.

—PAULA MARCHESI LENHARTSVILLE, PA

PREP: 35 MIN. + CHILLING
BAKE: 15 MIN./BATCH + COOLING
MAKES: 4 DOZEN

- 1¾ cups all-purpose flour
- ½ cup sugar
- ⅓ cup cornstarch
- ¼ cup vanilla chai tea latte mix
- 1 cup cold butter, cubed
- ½ teaspoon vanilla extract
- ¾ cup finely chopped almonds
- ⅓ cup miniature semisweet chocolate chips
- 4 ounces semisweet chocolate, melted

1. Place flour, sugar, cornstarch and latte mix in a food processor; pulse until blended. Add butter and vanilla; pulse until butter is the size of peas. Add the almonds and chocolate chips; pulse until blended.

2. Transfer to a lightly floured surface; knead until dough forms a ball. Divide dough into six portions; wrap each in plastic wrap. Refrigerate at least 30 minutes or until firm enough to roll.

3. Preheat oven to 375°. On a lightly floured surface, roll each portion of dough into a 5-in. circle. Cut into eight wedges. Place 2 in. apart on ungreased baking sheets.

4. Bake 15-18 minutes or until edges begin to brown. Cool 1 minute before removing from pans to wire racks. Drizzle with melted chocolate; let stand until set. Store in airtight containers.

BAKING MORSELS

Sprinkle with salt. Remove from pans to wire racks to cool completely.
TO MAKE AHEAD *Cookies can be stored for 1 week in an airtight container at room temperature.*

NO-BAKE FUDGY COCONUT COOKIES

My daughter works at a summer camp, so I send her these treats for the kids. She uses a coffee can she calls "The Wrangler Feeding Trough" in place of a cookie jar. The kids request these year after year.
—**SUE KLEMM** RHINELANDER, WI

PREP: 30 MIN. + CHILLING
MAKES: 3½ DOZEN

- 1½ cups sugar
- ⅔ cup 2% milk
- ½ cup baking cocoa
- ½ cup butter, cubed
- ½ teaspoon salt
- ⅓ cup creamy peanut butter
- 1 teaspoon vanilla extract
- 2 cups quick-cooking oats
- 1 cup flaked coconut
- ½ cup white baking chips
- 1 teaspoon shortening

1. In a large saucepan, combine the first five ingredients. Bring to a boil, stirring constantly. Cook and stir for 3 minutes.
2. Remove from heat; stir in peanut butter and vanilla until blended. Stir in oats and coconut. Drop mixture by tablespoonfuls onto waxed paper-lined baking sheets.
3. In a microwave, melt baking chips and shortening; stir until smooth. Drizzle over cookies; refrigerate until set. Store in airtight containers.

SALTED CARAMEL FUDGE DROPS

You can make this dough in advance, roll it into balls and freeze it for up to 3 months. That way, just bake the cookies as you need them.
—**CAROLE HOLT** MENDOTA HEIGHTS, MN

PREP: 20 MIN. • **BAKE:** 10 MIN./BATCH
MAKES: 4 DOZEN

- 6 ounces unsweetened chocolate
- ⅓ cup butter, cubed
- 1 package (17½ ounces) sugar cookie mix
- 1 large egg
- 1 can (14 ounces) sweetened condensed milk
- 1 teaspoon vanilla extract
- 48 caramel-filled chocolate candies
  Coarsely ground sea salt

1. Preheat oven to 350°. Melt the unsweetened chocolate and butter in a microwave; stir until smooth. Cool slightly. In a large bowl, beat cookie mix, egg, milk, vanilla and chocolate mixture. Drop by tablespoonfuls 2 in. apart on ungreased baking sheets.
2. Bake 8-10 minutes or until edges are set. Press a candy into the center of each cookie. Let stand 2 minutes.

No-Bake Fudgy
Coconut Cookies

CHOCOLATE LINZER COOKIES

Living in the town of North Pole, it's no surprise that I enjoy holiday baking! My mom and I used to make these cookies together. Now that I'm married and living in Alaska, I love to bake them for my own family. They remind me of home.

—**HEATHER PETERS** NORTH POLE, AK

PREP: 30 MIN. + CHILLING
BAKE: 10 MIN./BATCH + COOLING
MAKES: 2 DOZEN

- ¾ **cup butter, softened**
- 1 **cup sugar**
- 2 **large eggs**
- ½ **teaspoon almond extract**
- 2⅓ **cups all-purpose flour**
- 1 **teaspoon baking powder**
- ½ **teaspoon salt**
- ½ **teaspoon ground cinnamon**
- 1 **cup (6 ounces) semisweet chocolate chips, melted**
  Confectioners' sugar
- 6 **tablespoons seedless raspberry jam**

1. In a small bowl, cream butter and sugar until light and fluffy. Add eggs, one at a time, beating well after each addition. Beat in extract. Combine the flour, baking powder, salt and cinnamon; gradually add to creamed mixture and mix well. Refrigerate for 1 hour or until easy to handle.

2. Divide dough in half. On a lightly floured surface, roll out one portion to ⅛-in. thickness; cut with a floured 2½-in. round cookie cutter. Roll out remaining dough; cut with a 2½-in. floured doughnut cutter so the center is cut out of each cookie.

3. Place 1 in. apart on ungreased baking sheets. Bake at 350° for 8-10 minutes or until edges are lightly browned. Remove to wire racks to cool.

4. Spread melted chocolate over the bottoms of solid cookies. Place cookies with cutout centers over chocolate. Sprinkle with confectioners' sugar. Spoon ½ teaspoon jam in center of each cookie.

BIG & BUTTERY CHOCOLATE CHIP COOKIES

Our version of the classic cookie is based on a recipe from a bakery in California called Hungry Bear. It's big, thick and chewy—perfect for dunking.

—TASTE OF HOME TEST KITCHEN

PREP: 35 MIN. + CHILLING
BAKE: 10 MIN./BATCH
MAKES: ABOUT 2 DOZEN

- 1 **cup butter, softened**
- 1 **cup packed brown sugar**
- ¾ **cup sugar**
- 2 **large eggs**
- 1½ **teaspoons vanilla extract**
- 2⅔ **cups all-purpose flour**
- 1¼ **teaspoons baking soda**
- 1 **teaspoon salt**
- 1 **package (12 ounces) semisweet chocolate chips**
- 2 **cups coarsely chopped walnuts, toasted**

1. In a large bowl, beat butter and sugars until blended. Beat in eggs and vanilla. In a small bowl, whisk flour, baking soda and salt; gradually beat into butter mixture. Stir in chocolate chips and walnuts.

2. Shape ¼ cupfuls of dough into balls. Flatten each to ¾-in. thickness (2½-in. diameter), smoothing edges as necessary. Place in an airtight container, separating layers with waxed or parchment paper; refrigerate, covered, overnight.

3. To bake, place dough portions 2 in. apart on parchment paper-lined baking sheets; let stand at room temperature for 30 minutes before baking. Preheat oven to 400°.

4. Bake 10-12 minutes or until edges are golden brown (centers will be light). Cool on pans 2 minutes. Remove to wire racks to cool.

ALMOND CHOCOLATE CHIP COOKIES *Reduce vanilla to 1 teaspoon and add ¼ teaspoon almond extract. Substitute toasted almonds for the walnuts.*

BIG & BUTTERY WHITE CHIP COOKIES *Substitute white baking chips for the chocolate chips and toasted hazelnuts for the walnuts.*

BIG & BUTTERY CRANBERRY NUT COOKIES *Substitute dried cranberries for the chocolate chips.*

BIG & BUTTERY CHERRY CHOCOLATE CHIP COOKIES *Substitute 1 cup chopped dried cherries for 1 cup of the walnuts.*

NOTE *To toast nuts, bake in a shallow pan in a 350° oven for 5-10 minutes or cook in a skillet over low heat until lightly browned, stirring occasionally.*

PARCHMENT PAPER POINTERS

Parchment paper is excellent for lining baking sheets when making cookies, since it makes cleanup a snap. There's no right or wrong side for best baking results.

Chocolate-Cherry
Angel Cake

Cakes & Pies

CHOCOLATE-CHERRY ANGEL CAKE

Here's a cake that will catch the eye of all your guests. It's beautiful and ideal for parties or holidays. If you like chocolate and cherries together, you'll love this cake!
—BARBARA WHEELER ROYAL OAK, MI

PREP: 20 MIN.
BAKE: 45 MIN. + COOLING
MAKES: 16 SERVINGS

- 1 **package (16 ounces) angel food cake mix**
- ½ **cup finely chopped maraschino cherries**
- 1 **cup semisweet chocolate chips**
- 1 **tablespoon maraschino cherry juice**
- 2 **teaspoons strong brewed coffee**
- ½ **teaspoon vanilla extract**
- 1 **container (8 ounces) sour cream**
- 1 **container (8 ounces) frozen whipped topping, thawed Chopped walnuts, grated chocolate and additional maraschino cherries**

1. Prepare the cake mix batter according to package directions; fold in chopped cherries. Gently spoon into an ungreased 10-in. tube pan. Cut through batter with a knife to remove air pockets.
2. Bake on the lowest oven rack at 350° for 45-55 minutes or until lightly browned and entire top appears dry. Immediately invert the pan; cool completely, about 1 hour. Run a knife around side and center tube of pan. Cut cake horizontally into three layers.
3. For filling, in a small heavy saucepan, cook and stir the chocolate chips, cherry juice, coffee and vanilla over medium-low heat until melted.

Remove from the heat; stir in the sour cream.
4. To assemble, place one cake layer on a serving plate; spread with one half of the filling. Repeat layers. Top with remaining cake layer. Spread whipped topping over the top and sides of cake. Garnish with walnuts, chocolate and cherries. Refrigerate until serving.

CHOCOLATE LOVER'S CREAM PIE

We were immediately hooked once we saw that this recipe called for Nutella, the sweet hazelnut-cocoa spread. Finding true love in a pie has never been simpler.
—JENN STEWART LA VERGNE, TN

PREP: 20 MIN. + CHILLING
MAKES: 8 SERVINGS

- 2 **cups heavy whipping cream**
- 3 **tablespoons sugar**
- ½ **teaspoon vanilla extract**
- 1 **package (8 ounces) cream cheese, softened**
- ¾ **cup confectioners' sugar**
- ⅔ **cup Nutella**
- 1 **chocolate crumb crust (9 inches) Grated chocolate**

1. In a large bowl, beat cream until it begins to thicken. Add sugar and vanilla; beat until stiff peaks form.
2. In another bowl, beat cream cheese, confectioners' sugar and Nutella until smooth. Fold in half of the whipped cream. Spoon into crust. Spread the remaining whipped cream over top. Garnish with chocolate. Refrigerate for at least 1 hour. Store leftovers in the refrigerator.

TOFFEE POKE CAKE

This recipe is a favorite among family and friends. I enjoy making it because it's so easy. The oozing caramel tastes wonderful paired with the smooth chocolate cake.

—JEANETTE HOFFMAN OSHKOSH, WI

PREP: 25 MIN.
BAKE: 25 MIN. + CHILLING
MAKES: 15 SERVINGS

- 1 **package chocolate cake mix (regular size)**
- 1 **jar (17 ounces) butterscotch-caramel ice cream topping**
- 1 **carton (12 ounces) frozen whipped topping, thawed**
- 3 **Heath candy bars (1.4 ounces each), chopped**

1. Prepare and bake cake according to package directions, using a greased 13x9-in. baking pan. Cool on a wire rack.
2. Using the handle of a wooden spoon, poke holes in cake. Pour ¾ cup caramel topping into holes. Spoon the remaining caramel over cake. Top with whipped topping. Sprinkle with candy. Refrigerate cake for at least 2 hours before serving.

BROWNIE-PEPPERMINT ICE CREAM PIE

A decadent brownie crust is a perfect partner for refreshing peppermint ice cream. My guests have come to expect this make-ahead dessert.

—CAROL GILLESPIE CHAMBERSBURG, PA

PREP: 30 MIN. • **BAKE:** 35 MIN. + FREEZING
MAKES: 8 SERVINGS

- 1 **package fudge brownie mix (8-inch square pan size)**
- ½ **cup vanilla or white chips**
- ½ **cup 60% cacao bittersweet chocolate baking chips**
- ⅓ **cup caramel ice cream topping**
- 1 **pint peppermint ice cream, softened**
- 1 **cup heavy whipping cream**
- ¼ **cup confectioners' sugar**
- ⅛ **teaspoon peppermint extract**
- ¼ **cup crushed peppermint candies**

1. Prepare brownie batter according to package directions; stir in vanilla and bittersweet chips. Spread onto the bottom and up the sides of a greased 9-in. pie plate.
2. Bake at 350° for 35-40 minutes or until a toothpick inserted near the center comes out clean. Cool for 5 minutes. Gently press down center of crust if necessary. Cool completely on a wire rack.
3. Drizzle caramel topping over crust; spread evenly with ice cream. Cover and freeze for 4 hours or until firm.
4. Remove from freezer 10 minutes before serving. Meanwhile, in a small bowl, beat cream, confectioners' sugar and extract until stiff peaks form. Spread over ice cream; sprinkle with crushed peppermints.

Brownie-Peppermint
Ice Cream Pie

FROSTY COFFEE PIE

This pie was inspired by my husband, who loves coffee ice cream, and his mom, who makes a cool dessert using pudding mix. Cooking is a way I show others that I care for them.

—**APRIL TIMBOE** SILOAM SPRINGS, AR

PREP: 15 MIN. + FREEZING
MAKES: 8 SERVINGS

- ¼ **cup hot fudge ice cream topping, warmed**
- 1 **chocolate crumb crust (9 inches)**
- 3 **cups coffee ice cream, softened**
- 1 **package (5.9 ounces) instant chocolate pudding mix**
- ½ **cup cold strong brewed coffee**
- ¼ **cup cold 2% milk**
- 1¾ **cups whipped topping**
- 1 **cup marshmallow creme**
- ¼ **cup miniature semisweet chocolate chips**

1. Spread ice cream topping into crust. In a large bowl, beat the ice cream, dry pudding mix, coffee and milk until blended; spoon into crust.
2. In another bowl, combine whipped topping and marshmallow creme; spread over the top. Sprinkle with chocolate chips. Cover and freeze until firm.

CHOCOLATE CANNOLI CAKE ROLL

Creamy ricotta cheese filling with a hint of cinnamon rolls up beautifully in this chocolate cake.

—TAMMY REX NEW TRIPOLI, PA

PREP: 20 MIN. + CHILLING
BAKE: 15 MIN. + COOLING
MAKES: 12 SERVINGS

- 1 package (8 ounces) cream cheese, softened
- 2 cups ricotta cheese
- 1 cup confectioners' sugar
- 1 teaspoon vanilla extract
- ½ teaspoon ground cinnamon
- ½ cup miniature semisweet chocolate chips

CAKE
- 1¾ cups chocolate cake mix
- ⅓ cup water
- 2 tablespoons canola oil
- 3 large eggs

1. In a small bowl, beat cream cheese until fluffy. Add the ricotta cheese, confectioners' sugar, vanilla and cinnamon; beat until smooth. Stir in chips; refrigerate for 1 hour.

2. Preheat oven to 350°. Line a greased 15x10x1-in. baking pan with waxed paper and grease the paper; set aside. In a large bowl, combine the cake mix, water, oil and eggs; beat on low speed for 30 seconds. Beat on medium for 2 minutes. Pour into prepared pan. Bake 12-14 minutes or until the cake springs back when lightly touched. Cool for 5 minutes.

3. Invert onto a kitchen towel dusted with confectioners' sugar. Gently peel off waxed paper. Roll up cake in the towel jelly-roll style, starting with a short side. Cool completely on a wire rack.

4. Unroll cake; spread filling over cake to within ½ in. of edges. Roll up again. Place seam side down on a serving platter. Refrigerate cake for 2 hours before serving.

BAKING MORSELS

TRIPLE CHOCOLATE DREAM PIE

PREP: 30 MIN. + CHILLING
MAKES: 8 SERVINGS

- 1½ **cups graham cracker crumbs**
- 2 **tablespoons butter, melted**
- 1 **large egg white**

FILLING

- ⅔ **cup sugar**
- ⅓ **cup baking cocoa**
- 3 **tablespoons cornstarch**
- ⅛ **teaspoon salt**
- 2 **cups fat-free milk**
- 1 **large egg, beaten**
- ¼ **cup semisweet chocolate chips**
- 1 **teaspoon vanilla extract**

TOPPING

- 1½ **cups reduced-fat whipped topping**
- 1 **teaspoon grated chocolate**

1. Combine the graham cracker crumbs, butter and egg white; press onto the bottom and up the sides of a greased 9-in. pie plate. Bake at 375° for 6-8 minutes or until lightly browned. Cool on a wire rack.

2. For filling, in a large saucepan, combine the sugar, cocoa, cornstarch and salt. Stir in the milk until smooth. Cook and stir over medium-high heat until mixture is thickened and bubbly. Reduce the heat to low; cook and stir 2 minutes longer.

3. Remove from the heat. Stir a small amount of hot mixture into egg; return all to the pan, stirring constantly. Bring to a gentle boil; cook and stir for 2 minutes. Remove from the heat; stir in chocolate chips and vanilla.

4. Pour into crust. Refrigerate for at least 2 hours or until firm. Spread the whipped topping over filling; sprinkle with grated chocolate.

A fluffy chocolate pie always makes for an indulgent dessert. My light version lets you have this treat without any guilt. Sometimes I add a teaspoon of instant coffee granules to the sugar-cocoa mixture for a mocha pie.

—MARY ANN RING BLUFFTON, OH

BANANA CHIP CAKE

One of my favorite treats is Ben & Jerry's Chunky Monkey ice cream, so I decided to create a cake with the same flavors. The hardest part is waiting for it to cool!

—**BARBARA PRYOR** MILFORD, MA

PREP: 25 MIN. • **BAKE:** 40 MIN. + COOLING
MAKES: 16 SERVINGS

- 1 **package yellow cake mix (regular size)**
- 1¼ **cups water**
- 3 **large eggs**
- ½ **cup unsweetened applesauce**
- 2 **medium bananas, mashed**
- 1 **cup miniature semisweet chocolate chips**
- ½ **cup chopped walnuts**

1. In a large bowl, combine the cake mix, water, eggs and applesauce; beat on low speed for 30 seconds. Beat on medium for 2 minutes. Stir in the bananas, chips and walnuts.

2. Transfer to a 10-in. fluted tube pan coated with cooking spray and sprinkled with flour. Bake at 350° for 40-50 minutes or until a toothpick inserted near the center comes out clean. Cool cake for 10 minutes before removing from pan to a wire rack to cool completely.

Best Chocolate
Cake

BEST CHOCOLATE CAKE

A layered chocolate cake always impresses, no matter the occasion. One bite and you'll definitely agree!

—**ELVI KAUKINEN** HORSEHEADS, NY

PREP: 20 MIN.
BAKE: 20 MIN. + COOLING
MAKES: 16 SERVINGS

- ¾ cup butter, softened
- 2 cups sugar
- 3 large eggs
- 2 teaspoons vanilla extract
- 2 cups all-purpose flour
- ¾ cup baking cocoa
- 1 teaspoon baking soda
- ½ teaspoon salt
- ¼ teaspoon baking powder
- 1½ cups 2% milk

CHOCOLATE FROSTING

- 2 cups (12 ounces) semisweet chocolate chips
- ½ cup butter, cubed
- 1 cup (8 ounces) sour cream
- 4½ cups confectioners' sugar
  Chocolate curls, optional

1. Line three 9-in. round baking pans with waxed paper; grease and flour the pans and paper. Set aside.

2. In a large bowl, cream butter and sugar until light and fluffy. Add eggs, one at a time, beating after each addition. Beat in vanilla. Combine the flour, cocoa, baking soda, salt and baking powder; add to the creamed mixture alternately with milk, beating well after each addition.

3. Transfer to prepared pans. Bake at 350° for 20-25 minutes or until a toothpick inserted near the center comes out clean. Cool for 10 minutes before removing from pans to wire racks to cool completely.

4. For frosting, in a small heavy saucepan, melt chips and butter over low heat. Transfer to a large bowl; cool for 5 minutes. Stir in the sour cream. Gradually beat in confectioners' sugar until smooth. Spread between layers and over top and sides of cake. Garnish cake with chocolate curls if desired. Refrigerate leftovers.

BAKING MORSELS

CHOCOLATE ALMOND SILK PIE

This recipe is one I clipped years ago, and it was an instant hit with my husband and daughters. It's been in my recipe file ever since. The combination of chocolate and almond is absolutely heavenly.

—**DIANE LARSON** ROLAND, IA

PREP: 20 MIN.
COOK: 30 MIN. + COOLING
MAKES: 8-10 SERVINGS

- ⅔ **cup all-purpose flour**
- ¼ **cup butter, softened**
- 3 **tablespoons finely chopped almonds, toasted**
- 2 **tablespoons confectioners' sugar**
- ⅛ **teaspoon vanilla extract**

FILLING

- ¾ **cup sugar**
- 3 **large eggs**
- 3 **ounces unsweetened chocolate, coarsely chopped**
- ⅛ **teaspoon almond extract**
- ½ **cup butter, softened**
  Sweetened whipped cream and toasted sliced almonds, optional

1. In a small bowl, combine the first five ingredients. Beat on low speed until well combined, about 2-3 minutes. Press onto the bottom and up the sides of a greased 9-in. pie plate. Bake at 400° for 8-10 minutes or until golden. Cool on a wire rack.

2. For filling, combine sugar and eggs in a small saucepan until well blended. Cook over low heat, stirring constantly, until mixture coats the back of a metal spoon and reaches 160°. Remove from the heat. Stir in the chocolate and almond extract until smooth. Cool to lukewarm (90°), stirring occasionally.

3. In a large bowl, cream butter until light and fluffy. Add the cooled egg mixture; beat on high speed for 5 minutes. Pour into cooled pie shell. Refrigerate for at least 6 hours before serving. Garnish with whipped cream and almonds if desired. Refrigerate leftovers.

TOASTING NUTS

You can quickly toast nuts by using either the oven or stovetop. For the oven method, preheat oven to 350°. Spread the nuts in a 15x10x1-in. baking pan and bake for 5-10 minutes or until lightly browned. If toasting on the stovetop, simply heat a dry skillet (don't add oil) until hot, then pour the nuts in and spread them in a single layer. Stir frequently to keep the nuts from turning too brown. Cook for 3 to 5 minutes.

BOURBON CHOCOLATE-PECAN PIE

Don't have bourbon on hand? Use three tablespoons of melted butter in its place.
—**SARAH VARNER** SANTA RITA, GUAM

PREP: 20 MIN. • **BAKE:** 50 MIN.
MAKES: 10 SERVINGS

Pastry for single-crust pie (9 inches)
½ **cup miniature semisweet chocolate chips**
4 **large eggs, lightly beaten**
1 **cup corn syrup**
½ **cup sugar**
6 **tablespoons butter, melted**
¼ **cup packed brown sugar**
3 **tablespoons bourbon**
1 **tablespoon all-purpose flour**
3 **teaspoons vanilla extract**
1½ **cups chopped pecans, divided**

1. Roll out pastry to fit a 9-in. pie plate. Transfer pastry to pie plate. Trim pastry to ½ in. beyond edge of plate; flute edges. Sprinkle chocolate chips into pastry shell. Set aside.

2. In a large bowl, whisk the eggs, corn syrup, sugar, butter, brown sugar, bourbon, flour and vanilla until smooth. Stir in 1 cup chopped pecans. Pour into pastry shell; sprinkle with remaining pecans.

3. Bake at 350° for 50-60 minutes or until set. Cool on a wire rack. Store leftovers in the refrigerator.

RAISIN-NUT CHOCOLATE CAKE

My husband really enjoys this delightful cake. It's gorgeous enough for a special occasion, but it's also so good that you'll want to make it any day of the week.

—KAREN SUE GARBACK-PRISTERA
ALBANY, NY

PREP: 20 MIN.
BAKE: 40 MIN. + COOLING
MAKES: 16 SERVINGS

- ⅓ **cup butter, softened**
- 1 **cup packed brown sugar**
- 2 **large eggs**
- 1½ **cups unsweetened applesauce**
- ½ **cup plus 3 tablespoons brewed coffee, room temperature, divided**
- 2 **cups all-purpose flour**
- ¾ **cup plus 3 tablespoons baking cocoa, divided**
- 1½ **teaspoons ground cinnamon**
- 1 **teaspoon baking soda**
- 1 **teaspoon ground allspice**
- ½ **teaspoon salt**
- ¼ **teaspoon ground cloves**
- 1½ **cups raisins**
- ¾ **cup chopped walnuts**
- 1⅓ **cups confectioners' sugar**

1. In a large bowl, cream butter and brown sugar until well blended. Add eggs, one at a time, beating well after each addition. Beat in applesauce and ½ cup coffee. Combine the flour, ¼ cup baking cocoa, cinnamon, baking soda, allspice, salt and cloves; gradually beat into the creamed mixture until blended. Fold in raisins and walnuts.

2. Pour into a 10-in. fluted tube pan coated with cooking spray. Bake at 350° for 40-45 minutes or until a toothpick inserted near the center comes out clean. Cool for 10 minutes before removing from pan to a wire rack to cool completely.

3. In a small bowl, combine the confectioners' sugar and remaining baking cocoa and coffee; drizzle over cake.

CHERRY CHOCOLATE PECAN PIE

I'm a pie baker, and my family frequently requests this particular one. With the brandy-infused cherries and chocolate chips, it's an awesome twist on pecan pie.

—**SONYA LABBE** WEST HOLLYWOOD, CA

PREP: 25 MIN.
BAKE: 40 MIN. + COOLING
MAKES: 8 SERVINGS

- ¾ **cup dried cherries**
- ½ **cup brandy**

CRUST
- 1¼ **cups all-purpose flour**
- 1 **tablespoon sugar**
- ¼ **teaspoon salt**
- ¼ **cup canola oil**
- 3 **tablespoons 2% milk**

FILLING
- ⅓ **cup butter, softened**
- 1½ **cups sugar**
- 3 **large eggs**
- ¾ **cup all-purpose flour**
- ⅛ **teaspoon salt**
- 1 **cup chopped pecans**
- 2 **ounces semisweet chocolate, chopped**
  Chocolate whipped cream, optional

1. In a small bowl, combine cherries and brandy. Cover and refrigerate for 1 hour.

2. In a small bowl, combine the flour, sugar and salt. Combine oil and milk; using a fork, stir oil mixture into flour mixture just until blended. Pat evenly onto the bottom and up the sides of a greased 9-in. pie plate; set aside. Drain the cherries, reserving 1 tablespoon brandy; set aside.

3. For the filling, in a large bowl, cream butter and sugar until light and fluffy. Beat in the eggs and reserved brandy. Combine the flour and salt; gradually add to creamed mixture. Fold in the pecans, chocolate and cherries; pour into prepared pastry.

4. Bake at 325° for 40-45 minutes or until golden brown. Cover the edges with foil during the last 15 minutes to prevent overbrowning if necessary. Cool on a wire rack. Serve with whipped cream if desired. Refrigerate leftovers.

NOTE *For chocolate whipped cream, beat ½ cup heavy whipping cream until it begins to thicken. Add 2 tablespoons chocolate syrup and beat until stiff peaks form.*

QUICK PIE TOPPING

For an adults-only pie topping, try folding 2 tablespoons of Baileys Irish Cream, Kahlua or apricot brandy into an 8-ounce carton of thawed whipped topping.

½ cup dark chocolate chips
⅓ cup sugar
1 tablespoon grated orange peel
2 tablespoons orange liqueur, optional
   Pastry for double-crust pie (9 inches)

1. In a large bowl, combine the ricotta cheese, eggs, chocolate chips, sugar, orange peel and, if desired, orange liqueur.
2. Roll out half of the pastry to fit a 9-in. pie plate; transfer pastry to pie plate. Fill with ricotta mixture.
3. Roll out remaining pastry into an 11-in. circle; cut into 1-in.-wide strips. Lay half of the strips across the pie, about 1 in. apart. Fold back every other strip halfway. Lay another strip across center of pie at a right angle. Unfold strips over center strip. Fold back the alternate strips; place a second strip across the pie. Continue to add strips until pie is covered with lattice. Trim, seal and flute edges.
4. Bake at 425° for 40-45 minutes or until crust is golden brown. Refrigerate leftovers.

ORANGE CHOCOLATE RICOTTA PIE

The orange and chocolate flavors make a classic pairing in this traditional Italian dessert, served during the holidays and for special occasions.

—TRISHA KRUSE EAGLE, ID

PREP: 20 MIN. • **BAKE:** 40 MIN. + COOLING
MAKES: 8 SERVINGS

2 cartons (15 ounces each) whole-milk ricotta cheese
2 large eggs, lightly beaten

BAKING MORSELS

_____   _____
_____   _____
_____   _____
_____   _____
_____   _____
_____   _____
_____   _____
_____   _____

TRUFFLE CAKE WITH CANDY CANE CREAM

There's nothing sweeter than this cake with a dollop of peppermint topping.

—CRISTI KIRKHAM WEST JORDAN, UT

PREP: 35 MIN. • **BAKE:** 40 MIN. + CHILLING
MAKES: 16 SERVINGS

- 1 **cup graham cracker crumbs**
- 1 **cup chopped pecans, toasted and coarsely ground**
- 2 **tablespoons plus ¾ cup sugar, divided**
- ¼ **cup butter, melted**
- 16 **ounces semisweet chocolate, coarsely chopped**
- 1 **cup heavy whipping cream**
- 6 **large eggs**
- ⅓ **cup all-purpose flour**

CREAM

- 1 **cup heavy whipping cream**
- 2 **tablespoons sugar**
- 4 **candy canes, finely ground**
- ¼ **to ½ teaspoon peppermint extract, optional**

1. Combine the cracker crumbs, pecans, 2 tablespoons sugar and butter; press onto the bottom and 1½ in. up the sides of a greased 9-in. springform pan. Place pan on a baking sheet.

2. In a large saucepan, cook chocolate and cream over low heat until the chocolate is melted. Cool. In a large bowl, beat the eggs, flour and the remaining sugar on high speed until mixture is thick and lemon-colored, about 5 minutes. Gradually beat in chocolate mixture.

3. Pour batter into prepared crust. Bake at 325° for 40-45 minutes or until center is almost set. Cool on wire rack for 10 minutes. Carefully run a knife around edge of the pan to loosen; cool 1 hour longer. Refrigerate for 4 hours or overnight.

4. Beat cream and sugar until stiff peaks form; fold in ground candy and extract if desired. Serve with cake.

OREO CHEESECAKE PIE

This is so quick, you'll have it table-ready in less than 10 minutes. Who knew a recipe that only called for three ingredients could be so good?
—**CATHY SHORTALL** EASTON, MD

START TO FINISH: 5 MIN.
MAKES: 8 SERVINGS

- 1 **carton (24.3 ounces) Philadelphia ready-to-serve cheesecake filling**
- 1½ **cups coarsely crushed Oreos (about 12 cookies), divided**
- 1 **chocolate crumb crust (9 inches)**

In a large bowl, combine cheesecake filling and 1¼ cups crushed cookies. Spoon into crust; sprinkle with the remaining cookies. Chill until serving.

CHERRY COLA CAKE

Cherry cola and marshmallows make a lovely chocolate dessert. I sometimes like to top it with vanilla ice cream.
—**CHERI MASON** HARMONY, NC

PREP: 30 MIN.
BAKE: 25 MIN. + COOLING
MAKES: 12 SERVINGS

- 1½ **cups miniature marshmallows**
- 2 **cups all-purpose flour**
- 2 **cups sugar**
- 1 **teaspoon baking soda**
- 1 **cup butter, cubed**
- 1 **cup cherry-flavored cola**
- 3 **tablespoons baking cocoa**
- 2 **large eggs**
- ½ **cup buttermilk**
- 1 **teaspoon vanilla extract**

FROSTING

- ¾ **cup butter, softened**
- 1 **cup confectioners' sugar**
- 1 **jar (7 ounces) marshmallow creme**
- 2 **tablespoons frozen cherry-pomegranate juice concentrate, thawed**
- **Fresh sweet cherries with stems**

1. Preheat oven to 350°. Line bottoms of two greased 9-in. round baking pans with parchment paper; grease paper. Divide marshmallows between pans.
2. In a large bowl, whisk flour, sugar and baking soda. In a small saucepan, combine butter, cola and cocoa; bring just to a boil, stirring occasionally. Add to flour mixture, stirring just until moistened.
3. In a small bowl, whisk the eggs, buttermilk and vanilla until blended; add to the flour mixture, whisking constantly. Pour into prepared pans, dividing batter evenly. (Marshmallows will float to the top.)
4. Bake 25-30 minutes or until a toothpick inserted into center comes out clean. Cool in pans for 10 minutes before removing to wire racks; remove paper. Cool completely.
5. For frosting, in a small bowl, beat butter and confectioners' sugar until smooth. Beat in marshmallow creme and juice concentrate on low speed just until blended.
6. Place one cake layer on a serving plate; spread top with 1 cup frosting. Top with remaining cake layer; spread with remaining frosting. Decorate with sweet cherries.
NOTE *To frost sides as well as top of cake, double amounts for frosting.*

Cherry Cola Cake

CHOCOLATE FRUIT BASKET CAKE

Basic ingredients jazz up this easy cake, one that's sure to bring oohs and aahs! The berries on top make it irresistible.

—*TASTE OF HOME* TEST KITCHEN

PREP: 30 MIN. • **BAKE:** 25 MIN. + COOLING
MAKES: 12 SERVINGS

1 **package chocolate cake mix (regular size)**
1 **can (16 ounces) chocolate frosting**
11 **Kit Kat candy bars (1½ ounces each)**
2 **pounds fresh strawberries**
1 **pint fresh blueberries**
1 **pint fresh raspberries**
2 **tablespoons apricot preserves, warmed**
 Fresh mint leaves, optional

1. Prepare and bake cake according to package directions, using two greased 9-in. round baking pans. Cool cake for 10 minutes before removing from pans to wire racks to cool completely.

2. Spread frosting between layers and over top and sides of cake. Separate candy bars; lightly press onto sides of cake. Arrange berries on top; brush with preserves. Garnish with mint if desired.

HOW-TO *To keep the cake stand clean while frosting, line the edge with 3-in. strips of waxed paper. Center the first cake layer over the strips. When finished frosting, carefully remove strips one piece at a time.*

CHOCOLATE EGGNOG PIE

PREP: 45 MIN. + CHILLING
MAKES: 8 SERVINGS

- ½ cup all-purpose flour
- ⅓ cup ground walnuts
- 3 tablespoons brown sugar
- 1 tablespoon baking cocoa
- ¼ cup reduced-fat butter, melted

FILLING

- ½ cup sugar
- 2 tablespoons cornstarch
- 2 cups reduced-fat eggnog
- 2½ teaspoons unflavored gelatin
- ½ cup cold water, divided
- 2 tablespoons baking cocoa
- ¾ teaspoon rum extract
- 2 cups reduced-fat whipped topping
  Additional reduced-fat whipped topping, optional
  Ground nutmeg, optional

1. Preheat oven to 375°. In a small bowl, mix flour, walnuts, brown sugar and cocoa; stir in butter. Lightly coat hands with cooking spray; press the mixture into an ungreased 9-in. pie plate. Bake 8-10 minutes or until set. Cool completely on a wire rack.

2. For the filling, in a small heavy saucepan, mix sugar and cornstarch. Whisk in eggnog. Cook and stir over medium heat until thickened and bubbly. Reduce heat to low; cook and stir 2 minutes longer. Remove from heat.

3. In a microwave-safe bowl, sprinkle gelatin over ¼ cup cold water; let stand 1 minute. Microwave on high for 20 seconds. Stir and let stand 1 minute or until gelatin is dissolved. Stir into eggnog mixture.

4. Divide mixture in half. In a small bowl, whisk cocoa and remaining water until blended; stir into one half of the eggnog mixture. Stir rum extract into the remaining half. Refrigerate both mixtures, covered, until partially set.

5. Fold 2 cups whipped topping into rum-flavored portion; spoon into crust. Gently spread chocolate portion over top. Refrigerate, covered, at least 2 hours before serving. If desired, top with additional whipped topping and sprinkle with nutmeg.

> Reduced-fat eggnog spices this creamy pie just right, creating a refreshing treat at the end of a holiday meal.
>
> **—KERI WHITNEY** CASTRO VALLEY, CA

CHOCOLATE-BERRY CREAM PIES

There's so much chocolate to enjoy in this recipe! A chocolaty crust surrounds a raspberry-chocolate filling in this ice cream treat.

—**CLEO MILLER** MANKATO, MN

PREP: 15 MIN. + FREEZING
MAKES: 3 PIES (8 SERVINGS EACH)

- ½ gallon chocolate ice cream, softened
- 1 can (11½ ounces) frozen cranberry-raspberry juice concentrate, thawed
- 1 carton (16 ounces) frozen whipped topping, thawed, divided
- 3 chocolate crumb crusts (9 inches)
- 1 can (21 ounces) raspberry pie filling

1. In a large bowl, combine the ice cream and juice concentrate. Fold in 4 cups whipped topping. Spoon into crusts. Cover and freeze for 4 hours or until firm.

2. Remove pies from the freezer 15 minutes before serving. Garnish with raspberry filling and remaining whipped topping.

SPICED CHOCOLATE MOLTEN CAKES

Take some time to linger over this soothing dessert. There's nothing better than a chocolate cake with a warm melted center.

—**DEB CARPENTER** HASTINGS, MI

START TO FINISH: 30 MIN.
MAKES: 2 SERVINGS

- ¼ cup butter, cubed
- 2 ounces semisweet chocolate, chopped
- 1½ teaspoons dry red wine
- ½ teaspoon vanilla extract
- 1 large egg
- 1 teaspoon egg yolk
- ½ cup confectioners' sugar
- 3 tablespoons all-purpose flour
- ⅛ teaspoon ground ginger
- ⅛ teaspoon ground cinnamon
    Additional confectioners' sugar

1. In a microwave, melt butter and chocolate; stir until smooth. Stir in wine and vanilla.

2. In a small bowl, beat the egg, egg yolk and confectioners' sugar until thick and lemon-colored. Beat in the flour, ginger and cinnamon until well blended. Gradually beat in the butter mixture.

3. Transfer to two greased 6-oz. ramekins or custard cups. Place the ramekins on a baking sheet. Bake at 425° for 10-12 minutes or until a thermometer inserted near the center reads 160° and sides of cakes are set.

4. Remove from the oven and let stand for 1 minute. Run a knife around edges of ramekins; invert onto dessert plates. Dust with additional confectioners' sugar. Serve immediately.

CHOCOLATE-HAZELNUT CREAM PIE

We've all seen peanut butter pies, so why not be adventurous and try a Nutella pie? It's fabulous.

—ANNA SMITH NORTH SALT LAKE, UT

PREP: 20 MIN. + CHILLING • **BAKE:** 15 MIN.
MAKES: 8 SERVINGS

- **16 Oreo cookies**
- **¼ cup butter, melted**
- **1 package (8 ounces) cream cheese, softened**
- **¾ cup Nutella**
- **½ cup confectioners' sugar**
- **1 teaspoon vanilla extract**
- **1 cup heavy whipping cream**

TOPPING
- **¼ cup heavy whipping cream**
- **1 tablespoon light corn syrup**
- **2 teaspoons butter**
- **⅛ teaspoon salt**
- **2 ounces semisweet chocolate, finely chopped**
- **2 tablespoons chopped hazelnuts, toasted**

1. Place cookies in a food processor; cover and pulse for 1-2 minutes or until mixture resembles fine crumbs. Add butter; process until blended. Press crumb mixture onto the bottom and up the sides of a greased 9-in. pie plate.

2. Bake at 350° for 13-15 minutes. Cool on a wire rack for 30 minutes.

3. Meanwhile, in a large bowl, beat the cream cheese, Nutella, confectioners' sugar and vanilla until smooth.

4. In a small bowl, beat whipping cream until stiff peaks form; fold into cream cheese mixture. Pour into pie crust. Refrigerate for 30 minutes.

5. In a small saucepan over medium heat, bring the cream, corn syrup, butter and salt to a boil. Remove from the heat; add chocolate. Cover and let stand for 5 minutes; stir until smooth. Set aside to cool to room temperature. Spread over pie. Garnish with chopped hazelnuts. Chill for 1 hour.

Chocolate-Caramel
Dream Pie

CHOCOLATE-CARAMEL DREAM PIE

Chocolate, caramel and cream cheese come together to produce a pleasing pie, and adding the chocolate stars on top makes it perfect for a patriotic gathering. Make sure your guests save room for dessert!

—ANNA ROBB HARRISON, AR

PREP: 25 MIN. + CHILLING • **MAKES:** 8 SERVINGS

- 1½ cups crushed crisp ladyfinger cookies
- ⅓ cup butter, melted
- ½ cup Nutella
- ⅔ cup caramel ice cream topping
- 2 tablespoons plus 2 cups heavy whipping cream, divided
- 1½ cups slivered almonds
- 1 package (8 ounces) cream cheese, softened
- ⅓ cup plus 1 tablespoon confectioners' sugar, divided
- 1½ cups semisweet chocolate chips, melted
- 2 teaspoons vanilla extract
  Additional heavy whipping cream, whipped
  Chocolate stars for garnish, optional

1. Combine crushed cookies and butter; press onto the bottom and up the sides of a greased 9-in. pie plate. Refrigerate for 30 minutes.

2. Spread Nutella over crust. In a large bowl, combine caramel topping and 2 tablespoons cream; stir in almonds. Spoon over Nutella layer.

3. In a small bowl, beat cream cheese and ⅓ cup confectioners' sugar; stir in melted chocolate and vanilla until smooth. In a large bowl, beat remaining cream until stiff peaks form; fold into cream cheese mixture. Spread over caramel-almond layer.

4. Sprinkle with remaining confectioners' sugar. Garnish with additional whipped cream and chocolate stars if desired. Refrigerate for at least 1 hour before serving.

NOTE *This recipe was tested with Alessi crisp ladyfinger cookies. Kept refrigerated, this can be made the day before serving.*

BAKING MORSELS

BROWNIE CHEESECAKE SNICKERS PIE

This is the kind of treat you thought only existed in your dreams. Just as the name implies, it's a triple-threat dessert in a high deep-dish pie.

—**GENISE KRAUSE** STURGEON BAY, WI

PREP: 45 MIN.
BAKE: 20 MIN. + COOLING
MAKES: 10 SERVINGS

- ⅓ **cup butter, cubed**
- 1 **cup sugar**
- 2 **tablespoons water**
- 6 **ounces semisweet chocolate, chopped**
- 1 **teaspoon vanilla extract**
- 2 **large eggs**
- ¾ **cup all-purpose flour**
- ¼ **teaspoon baking soda**
- ⅛ **teaspoon salt**

CREAM CHEESE LAYER
- 10 **ounces cream cheese, softened**
- ⅓ **cup sugar**
- 1 **large egg, beaten**
- 1 **teaspoon vanilla extract**
- 4 **Snickers candy bars (2.07 ounces each), cut into ½-inch pieces**

GLAZE
- ½ **cup heavy whipping cream**
- 4 **ounces semisweet chocolate, chopped**

1. Preheat oven to 325°. In a heavy saucepan, bring butter, sugar and water to a boil, stirring constantly. Remove from the heat. Stir in the chocolate until melted; cool slightly. Stir in vanilla.

2. In a large bowl, beat eggs until lightly beaten. Gradually add the chocolate mixture; mix well. Combine the flour, baking soda and salt; gradually add to egg mixture. Spread into a greased 9-in. deep-dish pie plate. Bake 20 minutes. Cool on a wire rack 10 minutes.

3. Meanwhile, in a large bowl, beat cream cheese, sugar, egg and vanilla just until blended. Arrange candy bar pieces over brownie layer; spread cream cheese mixture over top. Bake 18-20 minutes or until top is set and edges are lightly browned. Cool on a wire rack for 1 hour.

4. For glaze, bring cream to a simmer; remove from heat. Add chocolate and stir until smooth. Cool 15 minutes; pour over pie. Refrigerate until serving.

TO MAKE AHEAD *Pie can be made a day in advance. Cover and refrigerate.*

MEASURING MADE EASY

Simplify your kitchen life by storing measuring cups inside sugar and flour containers. No last-minute rummaging through the drawers!

CHOCOLATE-RASPBERRY ANGEL FOOD TORTE

Here's a classic angel food cake dressed up in its fruity best. This no-fuss torte tastes as great as it looks.

—**LISA DORSEY** PUEBLO, CO

START TO FINISH: 20 MIN.
MAKES: 12 SERVINGS

- 1 **prepared angel food cake (8 to 10 ounces)**
- 1½ **cups heavy whipping cream**
- ¼ **cup confectioners' sugar**
- ¼ **cup baking cocoa**
- 1 **jar (12 ounces) seedless raspberry jam**
  Fresh raspberries and mint leaves

1. Split cake horizontally into four layers. In a large bowl, beat the cream, confectioners' sugar and cocoa until stiff peaks form.

2. To assemble, place one cake layer on a serving plate; spread with a third of the raspberry jam. Repeat layers twice. Top with remaining cake layer. Spread frosting over top and sides of cake. Chill until serving. Just before serving, garnish with raspberries and mint leaves.

FROZEN GRASSHOPPER PIE

When I first spread my cream-pie wings, this seemed like the right recipe to try for my chocolate-loving family. It's tailored for adult tastes, so I usually serve it after the kids have gone to bed.

—LORRAINE CALAND SHUNIAH, ON

PREP: 20 MIN. + CHILLING
COOK: 15 MIN. + FREEZING
MAKES: 8 SERVINGS

1¼ cups chocolate wafer crumbs
   (about 22 wafers)
¼ cup sugar
¼ cup butter, melted

FILLING

1 package (10 ounces) miniature
   marshmallows
⅓ cup 2% milk
¼ cup creme de menthe
2 tablespoons creme de cacao
¼ teaspoon peppermint extract,
   optional
2 cups heavy whipping cream
   Maraschino cherries and additional
   whipped cream, optional

1. In a small bowl, mix wafer crumbs and sugar; stir in butter. Press onto bottom and up sides of a greased 9-in. pie plate. Refrigerate 30 minutes.

2. Meanwhile, in a large saucepan, combine marshmallows and milk; cook and stir over medium-low heat 12-14 minutes or until smooth. Remove from heat. Cool to room temperature, stirring occasionally. Stir in liqueurs and, if desired, extract.

3. In a large bowl, beat cream until soft peaks form; fold in marshmallow mixture. Transfer to crust. Freeze 6 hours or until firm. If desired, top with cherries and additional whipped cream just before serving.

Frozen
Grasshopper Pie

ZUCCHINI CHOCOLATE CAKE WITH ORANGE GLAZE

This twist on a classic recipe has a rich chocolate taste, a hint of orange and a little crunch from the walnuts.

—BARBARA WORREL GRANBURY, TX

PREP: 20 MIN. • **BAKE:** 50 MIN. + COOLING
MAKES: 16 SERVINGS

- ½ **cup butter, softened**
- 1½ **cups sugar**
- 2 **large eggs**
- ¼ **cup unsweetened applesauce**
- 1 **teaspoon vanilla extract**
- 2½ **cups all-purpose flour**
- ½ **cup baking cocoa**
- 1¼ **teaspoons baking powder**
- 1 **teaspoon salt**
- 1 **teaspoon ground cinnamon**
- ½ **teaspoon baking soda**
- ½ **cup fat-free milk**
- 3 **cups shredded zucchini**
- ½ **cup chopped walnuts**
- 1 **tablespoon grated orange peel**

GLAZE
- 1¼ **cups confectioners' sugar**
- 2 **tablespoons orange juice**
- 1 **teaspoon vanilla extract**

1. Coat a 10-in. fluted tube pan with cooking spray and sprinkle with flour.
2. In a large bowl, cream the butter and sugar until light and fluffy. Add the eggs, one at a time, beating well after each addition. Beat in applesauce and vanilla.
3. Combine the flour, cocoa, baking powder, salt, cinnamon and soda; add to creamed mixture alternately with milk, beating well after each addition. Fold in the zucchini, walnuts and orange peel.
4. Transfer to prepared pan. Bake at 350° for 50-60 minutes or until a toothpick inserted near the center comes out clean.
5. Cool cake for 10 minutes before removing from pan to a wire rack to cool completely. Combine glaze ingredients; drizzle over cake.

DOUBLE CHOCOLATE SHEET CAKE

You can feed a big family with this chocolaty cake or bring it to a potluck or church supper. It's just the right dessert to satisfy any sweet tooth.

—BARBARA WALSH MURDOCK, NE

PREP: 25 MIN. • **BAKE:** 25 MIN. + COOLING
MAKES: 24 SERVINGS

- ½ cup butter, softened
- 2 cups sugar
- 2 large eggs
- 3 teaspoons vanilla extract
- 2 cups all-purpose flour
- 1 teaspoon baking soda
- ½ teaspoon salt
- 1 cup water
- ½ cup 2% milk
- 2 ounces unsweetened chocolate, melted and cooled

FROSTING
- 1 cup sugar
- ½ cup 2% milk
- ½ cup butter, cubed
- 2 tablespoons baking cocoa

1. In a large bowl, cream butter and sugar until crumbly. Add eggs, one at a time, beating well after each addition. Beat in vanilla. Combine the flour, baking soda and salt; add to creamed mixture alternately with water and milk. Beat in chocolate until combined.

2. Pour into a greased 15x10x1-in. baking pan. Bake at 325° for 25-30 minutes or until a toothpick inserted near the center comes out clean. Cool on a wire rack.

3. For frosting, in a small saucepan, combine the sugar, milk, butter and cocoa. Bring to a boil; cook and stir for 1 minute. Remove from the heat. Transfer to a bowl; stir occasionally until completely cooled. Beat until smooth; spread over cake.

BAKING MORSELS

CHOCOLATE & PEANUT BUTTER PUDDING PIE WITH BANANAS

I created this pie in tribute to Elvis, who was my favorite entertainer, and to Hershey, Pennsylvania, the town where I was born.
—**PENNY HAWKINS** MEBANE, NC

PREP: 25 MIN. + CHILLING • **BAKE:** 10 MIN.
MAKES: 8 SERVINGS

- **1   cup chocolate wafer crumbs (about 20 wafers)**
- **¼   cup butter, melted**
- **2   medium firm bananas**
- **¾   cup creamy peanut butter**
- **2   ounces semisweet chocolate, chopped**
- **2   cups cold 2% milk**
- **2   packages (3.4 ounces each) instant vanilla pudding mix**
- **2   cups whipped topping, divided**
- **2   tablespoons chopped salted peanuts**
  Peanut butter cups, optional

1. In a small bowl, mix wafer crumbs and butter; press onto the bottom and up the sides of an ungreased 9-in. pie plate. Bake at 350° for 8-10 minutes or until set. Cool completely on a wire rack.

2. Slice bananas; arrange on bottom of crust. In a microwave-safe bowl, combine peanut butter and chocolate; microwave on high for 1-1½ minutes or until blended and smooth, stirring every 30 seconds. Spoon over bananas.

3. In a large bowl, whisk milk and pudding mix for 2 minutes. Let stand for 2 minutes or until soft-set. Fold in 1 cup whipped topping; spread over chocolate mixture. Pipe the remaining whipped topping over edge. Refrigerate pie, covered, for at least 3 hours.

4. Sprinkle with peanuts just before serving. If desired, serve with cut-up peanut butter cups.

Chocolate & Peanut Butter
Pudding Pie with Bananas

Dark Chocolate
Carrot Cake

DARK CHOCOLATE CARROT CAKE

Carrot cake has a dark side—and it's delicious! Cream cheese and shredded carrots in the batter keep the cake moist, while toasted nuts and cinnamon boost the flavor.

—DARLENE BRENDEN SALEM, OR

PREP: 20 MIN.
BAKE: 25 MIN. + COOLING
MAKES: 16 SERVINGS

- 1 **package dark chocolate cake mix (regular size)**
- 4 **ounces cream cheese, softened**
- 1 **package (3.9 ounces) instant chocolate pudding mix**
- 1 **cup 2% milk**
- 3 **large eggs**
- 1 **teaspoon ground cinnamon**
- 3 **cups shredded carrots**
- 1 **cup chopped walnuts, toasted, divided**
- 2 **cans (16 ounces each) cream cheese frosting**

1. In a large bowl, combine the cake mix, cream cheese, pudding mix, milk, eggs and cinnamon; beat on low speed for 30 seconds. Beat on medium for 2 minutes. Stir in carrots and ½ cup walnuts. Pour into three greased and floured 8-in. round baking pans.
2. Bake at 350° for 25-30 minutes or until a toothpick inserted near the center comes out clean. Cool cake for 10 minutes before removing from pans to wire racks to cool completely.
3. Spread frosting between layers and over top and sides of cake. Sprinkle top with remaining walnuts. Store in the refrigerator.

CONTEST-WINNING GERMAN CHOCOLATE CREAM PIE

I've won a few awards in recipe contests over the years, but I was truly delighted when this luscious pie sent me to the finals of the Great American Pie Show in Branson, Missouri.

—MARIE RIZZIO INTERLOCHEN, MI

PREP: 20 MIN. • **BAKE:** 45 MIN. + COOLING
MAKES: 8 SERVINGS

Pastry for single-crust pie (9 inches)
4   ounces German sweet chocolate, chopped
¼   cup butter, cubed
1   can (12 ounces) evaporated milk
1½ cups sugar
3   tablespoons cornstarch
    Dash salt
2   large eggs
1   teaspoon vanilla extract
1⅓ cups flaked coconut
½   cup chopped pecans
TOPPING
2   cups heavy whipping cream
2   tablespoons confectioners' sugar
1   teaspoon vanilla extract
    Additional flaked coconut and chopped pecans

1. Line a 9-in. pie plate with pastry; trim and flute edges.

2. Place the chocolate and butter in a small saucepan. Cook and stir over low heat until smooth. Remove from the heat; stir in milk. In a large bowl, combine the sugar, cornstarch and salt. Add the eggs, vanilla and chocolate mixture; mix well. Pour into crust. Sprinkle with coconut and pecans.

3. Bake at 375° for 45-50 minutes or until a knife inserted near the center comes out clean. Cool completely on a wire rack.

4. For topping, in a large bowl, beat the cream until it begins to thicken. Add confectioners' sugar and vanilla; beat until stiff peaks form. Spread over pie; sprinkle with additional coconut and pecans. Refrigerate until serving.

DOUBLE-CHOCOLATE HOLIDAY PIE

Smooth and creamy, this velvety pie will be a change of pace on the dessert table. A hint of orange in the cranberry topping adds extra pizzazz that's just too tempting to resist.

—TASTE OF HOME TEST KITCHEN

PREP: 25 MIN. + CHILLING
MAKES: 8 SERVINGS

- ½ cup dark chocolate chips
- ¼ cup sweetened condensed milk
- 1 extra-servings graham cracker crust (9 ounces)
- 2 tablespoons plus ⅓ cup slivered almonds, divided
- 1 cup cold 2% milk
- 1 package (3.3 ounces) instant white chocolate pudding mix
- 1 envelope unflavored gelatin
- 2 cups heavy whipping cream, divided
- 2 tablespoons sugar
- ¼ teaspoon almond extract
- 1 can (14 ounces) whole-berry cranberry sauce
- ¼ teaspoon grated orange peel

1. Place the chocolate chips and milk in a small microwave-safe bowl. Microwave, uncovered, on high for 30-60 seconds or until chocolate is melted; stir until smooth. Spread into crust; sprinkle with 2 tablespoons slivered almonds.

2. In a large bowl, whisk milk and pudding mix for 2 minutes; set aside. In a small saucepan, sprinkle gelatin over ½ cup cream; let stand for 1 minute. Heat over low heat, stirring until the gelatin is dissolved. Remove from the heat.

3. In a large bowl, beat remaining cream until it begins to thicken. Add sugar and extract; beat until soft peaks form. Gradually beat in gelatin mixture. Fold into pudding. Pour into crust. Refrigerate for 4 hours or until firm.

4. Place cranberry sauce in a food processor; cover and process until blended. Stir in orange peel. Spoon over top; sprinkle with remaining almonds. Refrigerate leftovers.

MELTING 101

Water can make chocolate seize, so it's important to always use dry utensils and dishes when melting chocolate. Also, chocolate can scorch over high heat, so it's better to melt it slowly in the microwave or over low heat in a double boiler.

Raspberry
Sacher Torte

RASPBERRY SACHER TORTE

This torte looks like it took hours to make, but it has a surprisingly short list of ingredients. A small slice hits the spot.

—ROSE HOCKETT COLORADO SPRINGS, CO

PREP: 50 MIN. • **BAKE:** 25 MIN. + STANDING
MAKES: 12 SERVINGS

- 4 **large eggs, separated**
- 5 **tablespoons butter**
- ⅔ **cup sugar**
- 9 **ounces bittersweet chocolate, melted**
- ¾ **cup ground almonds**
- ¼ **cup all-purpose flour**
- ¼ **cup seedless raspberry jam**

GLAZE
- 3 **ounces bittersweet chocolate, chopped**
- 2 **tablespoons butter**

1. Place egg whites in a large bowl; let stand at room temperature for 30 minutes. In another large bowl, beat butter and sugar until crumbly, about 2 minutes. Add egg yolks and melted chocolate; beat on low speed just until combined. Combine almonds and flour; stir into butter mixture just until blended.

2. In another bowl, using clean beaters, beat egg whites until stiff peaks form; fold into batter. Transfer to a greased 9-in. springform pan. Bake at 350° for 25-30 minutes or until a toothpick inserted near the center comes out clean. Cool on a wire rack for 10 minutes. Carefully run a knife around edge of pan to loosen; remove sides of pan. Cool completely.

3. Spread jam over top of cake. For glaze, in a small saucepan, melt chocolate and butter; spread over jam. Let stand at room temperature for 1 hour or until set.

FREEZE OPTION *Bake the cake and let cool (do not top with jam); freeze in a heavy-duty resealable plastic bag for up to 3 months. When ready to use, thaw cake at room temperature overnight. Top with jam and glaze.*

BAKING MORSELS

3. Cook, covered, on high 2-2½ hours or until a toothpick inserted into cake portion comes out with moist crumbs. If desired, sprinkle with peanuts. Serve warm.

CHOCOLATE CARAMEL NUT CAKE

One of my cousins served this at our annual family reunion many years ago, and she was swamped with recipe requests. One taste will tell you why!

—FRIEDA MILLER BENTON HARBOR, MI

PREP: 15 MIN. • **BAKE:** 40 MIN.
MAKES: 20 SERVINGS

- 1 **package German chocolate cake mix (regular size)**
- 1 **package (14 ounces) caramels**
- ½ **cup evaporated milk**
- 6 **tablespoons butter, cubed**
- 1 **cup chopped pecans**
- 1 **cup (6 ounces) chocolate chips**
   Pecan halves for garnish, optional

1. Prepare cake according to package directions. Set aside half of batter; pour remaining batter into a greased and floured 13x9-in. baking pan.
2. Bake at 350° for 18 minutes. Meanwhile, in a small saucepan, melt the caramels, milk and butter. Remove from heat; stir in nuts. Pour over cake. Sprinkle with chocolate chips, then pour reserved batter over top.
3. Bake 20 minutes longer or until cake springs back when touched lightly. Cool on a wire rack. Cut into squares and top each with a pecan half if desired.

GOOEY PEANUT BUTTER-CHOCOLATE CAKE

Here in Wisconsin, winter weather is extreme. A hot dessert is the perfect way to warm up. I suggest sprinkling peanuts on top to complete the dish.

—LISA ERICKSON RIPON, WI

PREP: 20 MIN. • **COOK:** 2 HOURS
MAKES: 8 SERVINGS

- 1¾ **cups sugar, divided**
- 1 **cup 2% milk**
- ¾ **cup creamy peanut butter**
- 3 **tablespoons canola oil**
- 2 **cups all-purpose flour**
- ¾ **cup baking cocoa, divided**
- 3 **teaspoons baking powder**
- 2 **cups boiling water**
   Chopped salted peanuts, optional

1. In a large bowl, beat 1 cup sugar, milk, peanut butter and oil until well blended. In another bowl, whisk the flour, ½ cup cocoa and baking powder; gradually beat into the peanut butter mixture (batter will be thick). Transfer to a greased 5-qt. slow cooker.
2. In a small bowl, mix the remaining sugar and cocoa. Stir in water. Pour over batter (do not stir).

CHOCOLATE PARTY CAKE

Let this beautiful cake shine at your next gathering. Its luscious coffee-flavored icing really seals the appeal deal.
—GLORIA WARCZAK CEDARBURG, WI

PREP: 20 MIN. • **BAKE:** 35 MIN. + COOLING
MAKES: 12 SERVINGS

- 1 **package devil's food cake mix (regular size)**
- 1 **package (3.4 ounces) cook-and-serve chocolate pudding mix**
- 1 **envelope whipped topping mix (Dream Whip)**
- 1 **cup water**
- ¼ **cup canola oil**
- 4 **large eggs**

MOCHA RUM ICING

- 2 **tablespoons butter, softened**
- 2 **cups confectioners' sugar**
- ⅓ **cup baking cocoa**
- 2 **tablespoons refrigerated nondairy creamer**
- ½ **teaspoon rum extract**
- 2 **to 3 tablespoons brewed coffee Chopped pecans, optional**

1. In a large bowl, combine the first six ingredients; beat on low speed for 30 seconds. Beat on medium speed for 4 minutes. Pour into a greased and floured 10-in. fluted tube pan.

2. Bake at 350° for 35-40 minutes or until a toothpick inserted near the center comes out clean. Cool cake for 10 minutes before removing from pan to a wire rack to cool completely.

3. For icing, in a small bowl, beat the butter, confectioners' sugar, cocoa, creamer, extract and enough coffee to achieve desired drizzling consistency. Drizzle over cake. Garnish with pecans if desired.

Cherry-Chocolate
Cream Puffs

Bakeshop
Favorites

CHERRY-CHOCOLATE CREAM PUFFS

This fancy and fun chocolate-filled cream puff is perfect for cherry lovers.

—CHRISTOPHER FUSON MARYSVILLE, OH

PREP: 30 MIN. + COOLING
BAKE: 30 MIN. + COOLING
MAKES: 10 SERVINGS

- 1 **cup water**
- ⅓ **cup butter, cubed**
- 1 **tablespoon sugar**
- ⅛ **teaspoon salt**
- 1 **cup all-purpose flour**
- 4 **large eggs**

FILLING

- 1 **carton (8 ounces) frozen whipped topping, thawed**
- ½ **cup sugar**
- ¼ **cup 2% milk**
- 6 **ounces semisweet chocolate, chopped**
- ¾ **pound fresh or frozen pitted sweet cherries (thawed), coarsely chopped**
  Confectioners' sugar

1. Preheat oven to 400°. In a small saucepan, bring water, butter, sugar and salt to a rolling boil. Add flour all at once and beat until blended. Cook over medium heat, stirring vigorously until mixture pulls away from sides of pan and forms a ball. Remove from heat; let stand 5 minutes.

2. Add the eggs, one at a time, beating well after each addition until smooth. Continue beating until the mixture is smooth and shiny.

3. Drop dough by scant ¼ cupfuls 3 in. apart onto greased baking sheets. Bake 30-35 minutes or until puffed, very firm and golden brown. Remove to wire racks. Split puffs open. Pull out

and discard soft dough from inside tops and bottoms. Cool the puffs completely on a wire rack.

4. Let whipped topping stand at room temperature 30 minutes. Meanwhile, in a small saucepan, bring sugar and milk to a boil over medium heat; cook and stir until sugar is dissolved. Reduce heat to low; stir in the chocolate until melted. Transfer to a large bowl. Cool to room temperature, about 25 minutes, stirring occasionally. Fold in whipped topping.

5. Just before serving, fill each cream puff with a heaping tablespoonful of cherries; top with chocolate filling. Replace tops. Dust with confectioners' sugar. Refrigerate leftovers.

VANILLA CREAM PUFFS *Omit cherry-chocolate filling. In a bowl, whisk 1½ cups milk, 1 package (5.1 ounces) instant vanilla pudding mix and ½ teaspoon almond extract 2 minutes. Let stand 2 minutes or until soft-set. Fold in 4 cups whipped cream. Spoon into cream puffs.*

WHY CHOP CHOCOLATE?

When a *Taste of Home* recipe calls for the chocolate to be chopped before melting, it's because chocolate may burn if left in big pieces. Also, chopping the chocolate will ensure more even melting.

PRETTY POSY CUPCAKES

These cute cupcakes are a fun treat to make with kids. Simply bake and frost cupcakes, then decorate them with gumdrops and marshmallows.

—KAREN JERRELL NEW ALBANY, IN

PREP: 20 MIN.
BAKE: 20 MIN. + COOLING
MAKES: 2 DOZEN

- 1 **package chocolate cake mix (regular size)**
- 1 **can (16 ounces) chocolate frosting**
  Gumdrops and/or halved large marshmallows

1. Prepare cake batter for cupcakes according to package directions.
2. Fill paper-lined muffin cups two-thirds full. Bake at 350° for 20-22 minutes or until a toothpick inserted near the center comes out clean. Cool for 10 minutes before removing from pans to wire racks to cool completely.
3. Frost cupcakes. Use a dab of frosting to attach gumdrops and/or marshmallows to the top of each cupcake, forming a flower.

BOSTON CREAM CUPCAKES

I've always loved Boston cream bismarcks, so I put together this cupcake version.

—JEANNE HOLT MENDOTA HEIGHTS, MN

PREP: 25 MIN. • **BAKE:** 15 MIN. + COOLING
MAKES: ½ DOZEN

- 3 **tablespoons shortening**
- ⅓ **cup sugar**
- 1 **large egg**
- ½ **teaspoon vanilla extract**
- ½ **cup all-purpose flour**
- ½ **teaspoon baking powder**
- ¼ **teaspoon salt**
- 3 **tablespoons 2% milk**
- ⅔ **cup prepared vanilla pudding**
- ½ **cup semisweet chocolate chips**
- ¼ **cup heavy whipping cream**

1. In a small bowl, cream shortening and sugar until light and fluffy. Beat in egg. Beat in vanilla. Combine the flour, baking powder and salt; add to the creamed mixture alternately with milk, beating well after each addition.
2. Filled paper-lined muffin cups half full. Bake at 350° for 15-20 minutes or until a toothpick inserted near the center comes out clean. Cool for 10 minutes before removing from pan to a wire rack to cool completely.
3. Cut a small hole in the corner of a pastry or plastic bag; insert a small tip. Fill bag with pudding. Push the tip through the top to fill each cupcake.
4. Place chocolate chips in a small bowl. In a small saucepan, bring cream just to a boil. Pour over chocolate; whisk until smooth. Cool, stirring occasionally, to room temperature or until ganache thickens slightly, about 10 minutes. Spoon over cupcakes. Let stand until set. Store in an airtight container in the refrigerator.

Boston Cream
Cupcakes

DELICIOUS POTATO DOUGHNUTS

I first tried these tasty doughnuts at my sister's house and thought they were the best I've ever had. They're easy to make, and the fudge frosting tops them off well.

—PAT DAVIS BEULAH, MI

PREP: 20 MIN. • **COOK:** 40 MIN.
MAKES: 4 DOZEN

- 2 **cups hot mashed potatoes (with added milk and butter)**
- 2½ **cups sugar**
- 2 **cups buttermilk**
- 2 **large eggs, lightly beaten**
- 2 **tablespoons butter, melted**
- 2 **teaspoons baking soda**
- 2 **teaspoons baking powder**
- 1 **teaspoon salt**
- 1 **teaspoon ground nutmeg**
- 6½ **to 7 cups all-purpose flour**
  Oil for deep-fat frying

FAST FUDGE FROSTING
- 3¾ **cups confectioners' sugar**
- ½ **cup baking cocoa**
- ¼ **teaspoon salt**
- ⅓ **cup boiling water**
- ⅓ **cup butter, melted**
- 1 **teaspoon vanilla extract**

1. In a large bowl, combine potatoes, sugar, buttermilk and eggs. Stir in the butter, baking soda, baking powder, salt, nutmeg and enough of the flour to form a soft dough. Turn onto a lightly floured surface; pat out to ¾-in. thickness. Cut with a 2½-in. floured doughnut cutter.

2. In an electric skillet, heat 1 in. of oil to 375°. Fry the doughnuts for 2 minutes on each side or until browned. Place on paper towels.

3. For the frosting, combine the confectioners' sugar, cocoa and salt in a large bowl. Stir in the water, butter and vanilla. Dip tops of warm doughnuts in frosting.

HAZELNUT MOCHA ECLAIRS

Once you take a bite of these treats, especially the filling, you'll be in chocolate heaven. Enjoy them as a special meal finale or with afternoon coffee.

—CAROL WITCZAK TINLEY PARK, IL

PREP: 40 MIN.
BAKE: 25 MIN. + COOLING
MAKES: 14 SERVINGS

- ½ cup water
- ½ cup 2% milk
- ½ cup butter, cubed
- 1 tablespoon sugar
- ¼ teaspoon salt
- 1 cup all-purpose flour
- 4 large eggs

FILLING
- 1 tablespoon instant coffee granules
- 1 tablespoon boiling water
- 2 cups heavy whipping cream
- ¼ cup confectioners' sugar
- ½ cup chopped hazelnuts, divided

TOPPING
- ½ cup milk chocolate chips, melted

1. In a large saucepan, bring the water, milk, butter, sugar and salt to a boil. Add flour all at once and stir until a smooth ball forms. Remove from the heat; let stand for 5 minutes. Add eggs, one at a time, beating well after each addition. Continue beating until the mixture is smooth and shiny.

2. Transfer to a heavy-duty resealable plastic bag; cut a 1-in. hole in one corner of bag. Pipe 3-in. strips about 3 in. apart on greased baking sheets. Bake at 400° for 10 minutes. Reduce heat to 350°; bake 15-20 minutes longer or until golden brown.

3. Pierce side of each eclair with tip of knife. Cool on wire racks. Split eclairs open. Pull out and discard soft dough from inside tops and bottoms.

4. For filling, dissolve coffee granules in boiling water; cool. In a small bowl, beat cream and confectioners' sugar until stiff peaks form. Fold in coffee mixture and ¼ cup hazelnuts. Refrigerate.

5. Fill the eclairs just before serving; replace tops. Spread with melted chocolate. Sprinkle with remaining hazelnuts. Refrigerate leftovers.

BAKING MORSELS

CHOCOLATE RASPBERRY CUPCAKES

People have been known to finish these amazing cupcakes in two bites. But most prefer to savor each decadent morsel. You can store the snacks in the refrigerator for about a week or in the freezer for a month.

—**KIM BEJOT** AINSWORTH, NE

PREP: 30 MIN. + CHILLING
BAKE: 20 MIN. + COOLING
MAKES: 2½ DOZEN

- 1 cup baking cocoa
- 2 cups boiling water
- 1 cup butter, softened
- 2½ cups sugar
- 4 large eggs
- 2 tablespoons cold strong brewed coffee
- 2 teaspoons vanilla extract
- 2¾ cups all-purpose flour
- 2 teaspoons baking soda
- ½ teaspoon baking powder
- ½ teaspoon salt
- 1 cup seedless raspberry jam

FROSTING
- 1 can (13.66 ounces) coconut milk
- 1 package (12 ounces) dark chocolate chips
- ½ cup butter, cubed
- ⅓ cup confectioners' sugar
- 2 tablespoons coffee liqueur
- Toasted coconut

1. In a small bowl, combine cocoa and water; set aside to cool.

2. In a large bowl, cream butter and sugar until light and fluffy. Add eggs, one at a time, beating well after each addition. Beat in coffee and vanilla. Combine the flour, baking soda, baking powder and salt; add to the creamed mixture alternately with the cocoa mixture, beating well after each addition.

3. Fill paper-lined muffin cups two-thirds full. Drop raspberry jam by teaspoonfuls into center of each cupcake. Bake at 350° for 18-23 minutes or until a toothpick inserted into the cake portion comes out clean.

4. Cool for 10 minutes before removing from pans to wire racks to cool completely. Spread ½ teaspoon jam over each cupcake.

5. For frosting, spoon 1 cup cream from top of coconut milk and place in a small saucepan. Bring just to a boil; remove from the heat. Add chocolate chips; whisk until smooth. Stir in the butter, confectioners' sugar and coffee liqueur. Refrigerate for 1½ hours or until chilled.

6. In a small bowl, beat chocolate mixture until soft peaks form, about 15 seconds. Frost cupcakes. Garnish with coconut.

NO-BAKE CHOCOLATE-PECAN TARTLETS

I came up with these mini tarts at the last minute for a get-together. Turns out, they were a big hit! Now, I make them for our annual Teacher Taster's Choice and special family gatherings.
—**JOY JOHNSON** CULBERTSON, MT

PREP: 30 MIN. + STANDING • **COOK:** 5 MIN.
MAKES: 45 TARTLETS

- 1 **cup crushed vanilla wafers (about 30 wafers)**
- 1 **tablespoon spiced rum or 1 tablespoon water plus ½ teaspoon rum extract**
- 3 **tablespoons finely chopped pecans**
- ½ **cup sweetened condensed milk**
- ⅔ **cup semisweet chocolate chips**
- ½ **teaspoon vanilla extract**
- 3 **packages (1.9 ounces each) frozen miniature phyllo tart shells**
- 1 **cup coconut-pecan frosting**
  Additional finely chopped pecans

1. Place crushed wafers in a bowl. Drizzle with the rum and toss to combine. Let stand 15 minutes. Stir in 3 tablespoons pecans.

2. In a microwave-safe bowl, microwave milk, covered, on high for 15 seconds. Stir in chocolate chips and vanilla; microwave 15-30 seconds longer or until blended, stirring twice. Stir into wafer mixture.

3. Place tart shells on a serving plate. Fill each with 1 teaspoon of wafer mixture; top each with 1 teaspoon of frosting. Sprinkle with additional pecans. Refrigerate leftovers.

NOTE *This recipe was tested in a 1,100-watt microwave.*

Truffle Chocolate
Cupcakes

TRUFFLE CHOCOLATE CUPCAKES

I like food with an unexpected twist, like these cupcakes with a creamy chocolate truffle center. My kids love to get involved with preparing them, but I have to make sure there are enough truffles left to actually fill the cupcakes!

—**AMANDA NOLL** SPANAWAY, WA

PREP: 40 MIN. + CHILLING
BAKE: 20 MIN. + COOLING • **MAKES:** 2 DOZEN

- 1½ cups semisweet chocolate chips
- ½ cup plus 2 tablespoons sweetened condensed milk
- 1 teaspoon butter
- 2 teaspoons vanilla extract

CUPCAKES

- 1 package devil's food cake mix (regular size)
- 4 large eggs
- 1 cup (8 ounces) sour cream
- ¾ cup canola oil
- ½ cup water
- 2 teaspoons vanilla extract
- 1 cup heavy whipping cream, whipped, optional

1. For truffles, in a small saucepan, melt the chocolate, milk and butter over low heat; stir until blended. Remove from the heat. Stir in vanilla. Transfer to a small bowl; cover and refrigerate until firm, about 1 hour. Roll into twenty-four 1-in. balls; chill 1 hour longer.

2. For cupcakes, in a large bowl, combine cake mix, eggs, sour cream, oil, water and vanilla; beat on low speed for 30 seconds. Beat on medium for 2 minutes.

3. Fill paper-lined muffin cups one-third full. Drop a truffle into the center of each cupcake. Top with remaining batter. Bake at 350° for 17-22 minutes or until a toothpick inserted near the center comes out clean.

4. Cool for 10 minutes before removing from pans to wire racks to cool completely. Top with whipped cream if desired.

BAKING MORSELS

_____
_____
_____
_____
_____
_____
_____
_____
_____
_____
_____
_____
_____
_____
_____
_____
_____
_____
_____
_____
_____
_____
_____
_____
_____
_____
_____
_____
_____
_____
_____
_____
_____
_____
_____

CARAMEL CASHEW CAKE POPS

Nothing beats the combination of buttery caramel and rich cashews. Add it to a chocolaty cake pop and you have one irresistible little snack.
—*TASTE OF HOME* TEST KITCHEN

PREP: 1½ HOURS + CHILLING
MAKES: 4 DOZEN

- 1 **package chocolate cake mix (regular size)**
- ¾ **cup dulce de leche**
- 48 **lollipop sticks**
- 2½ **pounds milk chocolate candy coating, coarsely chopped**
  Chopped cashews

1. Prepare and bake the cake mix according to package directions, using a greased 13x9-in. baking pan. Cool completely on a wire rack.

2. Crumble cake into a large bowl. Add dulce de leche and mix well. Shape into 1-in. balls. Place on baking sheets; insert sticks. Freeze for at least 2 hours or refrigerate for at least 3 hours or until cake balls are firm.

3. In a microwave, melt candy coating. Dip each cake ball into coating; allow excess to drip off. Coat with cashews. Insert cake pops into a foam block to stand. Let stand until set.

NOTE *This recipe was tested with Nestle La Lechera dulce de leche; look for it in the international foods section. If using Eagle Brand dulce de leche (caramel flavored sauce), thicken according to package directions before using.*

Caramel Cashew
Cake Pops

BUYING CANDY COATING

Candy coating—sometimes called almond bark or dipping or confectionery coating—is available in large individual blocks, packages of flat disks or chips and boxes of individually wrapped 1-ounce squares.

DARK CHOCOLATE BACON CUPCAKES

I accepted a friendly challenge to use bacon in a cupcake recipe, and I was thrilled with the result. Use extra-smoky bacon to really get the salty, rich flavor.

—**SANDY PLOY** WHITEFISH BAY, WI

PREP: 25 MIN. • **BAKE:** 20 MIN. + COOLING
MAKES: 22 CUPCAKES

- 2 **cups sugar**
- 1 **cup buttermilk**
- 2 **large eggs**
- ½ **cup canola oil**
- ½ **cup strong brewed coffee**
- 2 **cups all-purpose flour**
- ¾ **cup plus 1 tablespoon baking cocoa, divided**
- 1¼ **teaspoons baking powder**
- ½ **teaspoon sea salt**
- ¼ **teaspoon baking soda**
- ¾ **pound bacon strips, cooked and crumbled, divided**
- 1 **can (16 ounces) chocolate frosting**

1. In a large bowl, beat the sugar, buttermilk, eggs, oil and coffee until well blended. In a small bowl, combine the flour, ¾ cup cocoa, baking powder, salt and baking soda; gradually beat into sugar mixture until blended. Stir in two-thirds of the bacon.

2. Fill paper-lined muffin cups two-thirds full. Bake at 375° for 18-22 minutes or until a toothpick inserted near the center comes out clean. Cool for 10 minutes before removing from pans to wire racks to cool completely.

3. Frost cupcakes. Sprinkle with remaining bacon; dust with remaining cocoa. Refrigerate leftovers.

I WANT S'MORE MUFFINS

With a fluffy marshmallow creme center and s'mores taste, these fun muffins will bring back fond childhood memories.

—SALLY SIBTHORPE SHELBY TOWNSHIP, MI

PREP: 20 MIN. • **BAKE:** 15 MIN.
MAKES: 6 MUFFINS

- 3 **tablespoons butter, softened**
- ¼ **cup packed brown sugar**
- 4 **teaspoons sugar**
- 1 **large egg**
- ⅓ **cup sour cream**
- 3 **tablespoons 2% milk**
- ⅔ **cup all-purpose flour**
- ½ **cup graham cracker crumbs**
- ¼ **teaspoon salt**
- ¼ **teaspoon baking powder**
- ¼ **teaspoon ground cinnamon**
- ⅛ **teaspoon baking soda**
- ⅓ **cup milk chocolate chips**
- 6 **tablespoons marshmallow creme**

1. In a small bowl, cream butter and sugars until light and fluffy. Beat in the egg, then the sour cream and milk. Combine the flour, graham cracker crumbs, salt, baking powder, cinnamon and baking soda; beat into creamed mixture until moistened. Fold in the chocolate chips.

2. Coat six muffin cups with cooking spray; fill one-fourth full with batter. Spoon 1 tablespoon marshmallow creme into each muffin cup. Top with remaining batter.

3. Bake at 400° for 14-16 minutes or until a toothpick inserted near the center comes out clean. Cool for 5 minutes before removing from pan to a wire rack. Serve warm.

CHOCOLATE CHIP MINI MUFFINS

I bake a lot of different muffins, but this is the recipe I use the most.

—JOANNE SHEW CHUK ST. BENEDICT, SK

PREP: 15 MIN. • **BAKE:** 10 MIN.
MAKES: ABOUT 3 DOZEN

- ½ **cup sugar**
- ¼ **cup shortening**
- 1 **large egg**
- ½ **cup 2% milk**
- ½ **teaspoon vanilla extract**
- 1 **cup all-purpose flour**
- ½ **teaspoon baking soda**
- ½ **teaspoon baking powder**
- ¼ **teaspoon salt**
- ⅔ **cup miniature semisweet chocolate chips**

1. In a large bowl, cream sugar and shortening until light and fluffy. Beat in egg, then milk and vanilla. Combine flour, baking soda, baking powder and salt; add to creamed mixture just until combined. Fold in the chocolate chips.

2. Spoon about 1 tablespoon of batter into each greased or paper-lined mini muffin cup. Bake at 375° for 10-13 minutes or until a toothpick inserted near center comes out clean. Cool in pans for 5 minutes before removing to wire racks. Serve warm.

Black Bottom
Cupcakes

BLACK BOTTOM CUPCAKES

This recipe's been in our family for years, but these cupcakes still go quickly each time I make them. So I always double or triple the ingredients to keep up with the demand! You'll experience it firsthand when you bake up a batch.

—JULIE BRICELAND WINDSOR, PA

PREP: 20 MIN. • **BAKE:** 20 MIN. + COOLING
MAKES: 20-24 CUPCAKES

FILLING
- 1 **package (8 ounces) cream cheese, softened**
- ⅓ **cup sugar**
- 1 **large egg**
- ⅛ **teaspoon salt**
- 1 **cup (6 ounces) semisweet chocolate chips**

CUPCAKES
- 1 **cup sugar**
- 1 **cup water**
- ⅓ **cup vegetable oil**
- 1 **large egg**
- 1 **tablespoon white vinegar**
- 1 **teaspoon vanilla extract**
- 1½ **cups all-purpose flour**
- ¼ **cup baking cocoa**
- 1 **teaspoon baking soda**
- ½ **teaspoon salt**

TOPPING
- **Sugar**
- **Chopped almonds, optional**

1. In a small bowl, beat the cream cheese, sugar, egg and salt until smooth. Stir in chips; set aside.

2. For cupcakes, in a large bowl, beat the sugar, water, oil, egg, vinegar and vanilla until well blended. Combine the flour, cocoa, baking soda and salt; gradually beat into the egg mixture until blended.

3. Fill paper-lined muffin cups half full with chocolate batter. Drop a heaping tablespoonful of cream cheese mixture in center of batter of each cupcake. Sprinkle with sugar and chopped almonds if desired.

4. Bake at 350° for 18-20 minutes or until a toothpick inserted into the cake portion comes out clean. Cool in pans for 10 minutes before removing the cupcakes to racks to cool completely. Refrigerate leftovers.

ALMOND-CHOCOLATE CRESCENTS

These breakfast rolls are yummy enough to also be a dessert. They look extra-special with a drizzle of melted chocolate.

—ROXANNE OBRIEN LYNDHURST, VA

START TO FINISH: 30 MIN.
MAKES: 8 ROLLS

- ¼ **cup almond paste**
- ¾ **cup semisweet chocolate chips**
- 1 **tablespoon shortening**
- 1 **tube (8 ounces) refrigerated crescent rolls**

1. Divide almond paste into eight portions; shape each into a small log. Set aside. In a microwave, melt chocolate chips and shortening; stir until smooth.

2. Unroll crescent dough; separate into triangles. Spread each with 1 tablespoon chocolate mixture; set aside remaining mixture for drizzling. Place one portion of almond paste at wide end of each triangle. Roll up and place point side down 2 in. apart on an ungreased baking sheet; curve ends to form a crescent.

3. Bake at 375° for 11-13 minutes or until golden brown. Remove to wire rack to cool completely. Drizzle with reserved chocolate mixture.

Apricot
Cheesecake Tarts

APRICOT CHEESECAKE TARTS

Dark chocolate and apricots create a flavor combo in these tiny cheesecakes that's too good to pass up.

—ALICIA MONTALVO PAGAN
NEW BEDFORD, MA

PREP: 30 MIN. + CHILLING
MAKES: 15 TARTLETS

- 3 **ounces bittersweet chocolate, chopped**
- ½ **teaspoon shortening**
- 1 **package (1.9 ounces) frozen miniature phyllo tart shells**
- 1 **package (3 ounces) cream cheese, softened**
- 2 **tablespoons confectioners' sugar**
- 2 **tablespoons sour cream**
- 2 **teaspoons apricot nectar**
- 3 **dried apricots, cut into thin strips**
- 1 **to 1½ teaspoons grated chocolate**

1. In a microwave, melt bittersweet chocolate and shortening; stir until smooth. Brush over the bottom and up the sides of tart shells. Refrigerate for 15 minutes or until chocolate is set.

2. Meanwhile, in a small bowl, beat cream cheese and confectioners' sugar until smooth. Beat in sour cream and apricot nectar. Spoon into shells. Cover and chill for at least 20 minutes. Just before serving, top with apricot strips and grated chocolate.

PIZZELLE CANNOLI

We made two Italian treats into one with beautiful pizzelle cookies wrapped around a cannoli filling.
—*TASTE OF HOME* TEST KITCHEN

PREP: 45 MIN. + COOLING • **COOK:** 5 MIN./BATCH
MAKES: 12 FILLED PIZZELLE

- 1 **large egg**
- ¼ **cup sugar**
- ¼ **cup butter, melted**
- ½ **teaspoon vanilla extract**
- ¼ **teaspoon grated lemon peel**
- ⅛ **teaspoon almond extract**
- ½ **cup all-purpose flour**
- ¼ **teaspoon baking powder**

FILLING
- ¾ **cup sugar**
- 3 **tablespoons cornstarch**
- 1 **cup milk**
- 1⅛ **teaspoons vanilla extract**
- 1 **drop cinnamon oil, optional**
- 1¾ **cups ricotta cheese**
- 1 **milk chocolate candy bar with almonds (4¼ ounces), chopped**
- ½ **cup chopped pistachios**

1. In a large bowl, beat the egg, sugar, butter, vanilla, lemon peel and almond extract until blended. Combine flour and baking powder; stir into egg mixture and mix well.

2. Bake in a preheated pizzelle iron according to manufacturer's directions until golden brown. Remove cookies and immediately shape into tubes. Place on wire racks to cool.

3. In a small saucepan, combine the sugar and cornstarch. Stir in milk until smooth. Bring to a boil; cook and stir mixture for 2 minutes or until thickened. Stir in vanilla and cinnamon oil if desired. Cool completely.

4. In a large bowl, beat the ricotta cheese until smooth. Gradually beat in the custard mixture. Fold in chocolate. Spoon or pipe into shells. Dip each side in pistachios. Serve immediately. Refrigerate leftovers.

Pizzelle Cannoli

Raspberry Truffle
Cake Pops

RASPBERRY TRUFFLE CAKE POPS

Rich chocolate with a hint of raspberry liqueur—it doesn't get any better than this!

—*TASTE OF HOME* **TEST KITCHEN**

PREP: 1½ HOURS + FREEZING
MAKES: 4 DOZEN

- 1 **package white cake mix (regular size)**
- ½ **cup canned vanilla frosting**
- ⅓ **cup seedless raspberry jam, melted**
- 2 **to 3 tablespoons raspberry liqueur**
  Red food coloring, optional
- 48 **lollipop sticks**
- 2½ **pounds dark chocolate candy coating, chopped**
  Pink candy coating, chopped
  Pink sprinkles and decorative sugar, optional

1. Prepare and bake the cake mix according to package directions, using a greased 13x9-in. baking pan. Cool completely on a wire rack.
2. Crumble cake into a large bowl. Add the frosting, jam, liqueur and food coloring if desired; mix well. Shape into 1-in. balls. Place on baking sheets; insert sticks. Freeze for at least 2 hours or refrigerate for at least 3 hours or until cake balls are firm.
3. In a microwave, melt dark candy coating. Dip each cake pop in coating; allow excess to drip off. Insert cake pops into a foam block to stand. Melt pink candy coating; drizzle over cake pops. Decorate some cake pops with sprinkles and sugar if desired. Let stand until set.

CHOCOLATE CINNAMON DOUGHNUTS

These doughnuts are a favorite of our three children. I usually prep them at night, then roll them out and fry in the morning.

—**JUDI EAKER** CHAFFEE, MO

PREP: 20 MIN. + CHILLING • **COOK:** 25 MIN.
MAKES: 2 DOZEN

- 2 **large eggs, beaten**
- 1¼ **cups sugar**
- ¼ **cup vegetable oil**
- 1 **teaspoon vanilla extract**
- 4 **cups all-purpose flour**
- ⅓ **cup baking cocoa**
- 4 **teaspoons baking powder**
- 1 **teaspoon ground cinnamon**
- ¾ **teaspoon salt**
- ¼ **teaspoon baking soda**
- ¾ **cup buttermilk**
  Oil or shortening for deep-fat frying

GLAZE
- 4 **cups sifted confectioners' sugar**
- 1 **teaspoon vanilla extract**
- ½ **teaspoon ground cinnamon**
- 6 **tablespoons milk**

1. In a bowl, beat eggs. Add sugar and beat until mixture is thickened and lemon-colored. Stir in oil and vanilla.
2. In another bowl, combine the flour, cocoa, baking powder, cinnamon, salt and baking soda. Add to egg mixture alternately with buttermilk. Chill.
3. Divide dough in half; refrigerate one portion. On a lightly floured surface, roll remaining dough to ½-in. thickness. Cut with a 2½-in. floured doughnut cutter. Repeat with the remaining dough. Heat oil to 375°; fry doughnuts in batches for 3 minutes, turning once. Drain on paper towels.
4. Combine glaze ingredients and dip tops of warm doughnuts.

MINIATURE NAPOLEONS

Looking for an elegant sweet to serve at your gathering or cocktail party? These bite-size desserts are easy to enjoy while mingling.

—*TASTE OF HOME* TEST KITCHEN

PREP: 30 MIN. + CHILLING
BAKE: 10 MIN. + FREEZING
MAKES: 4½ DOZEN

- 6 **tablespoons sugar**
- 2 **tablespoons cornstarch**
- ¼ **teaspoon salt**
- 1 **cup 2% milk**
- 1 **large egg yolk, beaten**
- 2 **tablespoons butter, divided**
- ½ **teaspoon vanilla extract**
- 1 **sheet frozen puff pastry, thawed**
- ½ **cup heavy whipping cream**
- 2 **ounces semisweet chocolate, chopped**

1. In a small saucepan, combine the sugar, cornstarch and salt. Stir in milk until smooth. Cook and stir mixture over medium heat until thickened and bubbly. Reduce heat; cook and stir 1 minute longer.

2. Remove from the heat. Stir a small amount of hot mixture into the egg yolk; return all to the pan, stirring constantly. Bring to a gentle boil; cook and stir 1 minute longer. Remove from the heat. Stir in 1 tablespoon butter and the vanilla. Cool to room temperature without stirring. Refrigerate custard until chilled.

3. Unfold puff pastry; place on an ungreased baking sheet. Prick dough thoroughly with a fork. Bake according to package directions. Remove to a wire rack to cool.

4. In a small bowl, beat cream until stiff peaks form. Fold into custard. Use a fork to split the pastry in half horizontally. Spread filling over the bottom half; replace top. Cover and freeze for 4 hours or until firm.

5. Cut into 1½x1-in. rectangles. In a microwave, melt the chocolate and remaining butter; stir until smooth. Drizzle over the pastries. Freeze until serving.

HANDLE WITH CARE

Thaw frozen puff pastry at room temperature for about 20 minutes before handling. Handle the puff pastry sheets as little as possible to avoid stretching or tearing.

PINEAPPLE MARZIPAN CUPCAKES

Pairing marzipan with pineapple may seem unusual, but it's so yummy. I've also made this recipe in a loaf pan.

—**JOHNNA JOHNSON** SCOTTSDALE, AZ

PREP: 30 MIN. • **BAKE:** 20 MIN. + COOLING
MAKES: 16 CUPCAKES

- ¾ **cup butter, softened**
- 1 **package (7 ounces) marzipan, crumbled**
- ½ **cup sugar**
- ¼ **cup packed brown sugar**
- 3 **large eggs**
- 1 **teaspoon vanilla extract**
- 2 **cups all-purpose flour**
- 2 **teaspoons baking powder**
- 1 **can (8 ounces) crushed pineapple, drained**

TOPPING

- 8 **ounces semisweet chocolate, chopped**
- 2 **tablespoons butter**
   Pineapple tidbits, patted dry

1. Preheat oven to 350°. Line 16 muffin cups with paper or foil liners.
2. In a large bowl, beat the butter, marzipan and sugars until blended. Add eggs, one at a time, beating well after each addition. Beat in vanilla. In another bowl, whisk flour and baking powder; gradually beat into butter mixture. Fold in crushed pineapple.
3. Fill prepared cups two-thirds full. Bake for 20-25 minutes or until a toothpick inserted into center comes out clean. Cool in pans for 10 minutes before removing cupcakes to wire racks to cool completely.
4. In a small heavy saucepan, melt the chocolate and butter over very low heat; stir until smooth. Cool slightly until mixture thickens to a spreading consistency. Spread over cupcakes. Top with pineapple bits.

CHOCOLATE-ORANGE CREAM PUFFS

Here's a triple treat for chocolate lovers: chocolate cream puffs with a velvety chocolate-orange filling and topped with a from-scratch chocolate syrup. Yum!

—**AGNES WARD** STRATFORD, ON

PREP: 35 MIN. • **BAKE:** 20 MIN. + COOLING
MAKES: 2 DOZEN

- 1 **cup water**
- ½ **cup butter, cubed**
- 1 **ounce semisweet chocolate, chopped**
- ¼ **teaspoon salt**
- 1 **cup all-purpose flour**
- 4 **large eggs**

CHOCOLATE ORANGE FILLING

- 2 **cups (12 ounces) semisweet chocolate chips**
- ⅔ **cup reduced-fat evaporated milk**
- 2 **tablespoons orange marmalade**
- 2 **tablespoons orange liqueur**
- 4 **cups whipped topping**

CHOCOLATE SYRUP

- ½ **cup sugar**
- ¼ **cup baking cocoa**
- 1 **tablespoon cornstarch**
  Dash salt
- 1 **cup water**
- 1 **teaspoon vanilla extract**

1. In a large saucepan, bring the water, butter, chocolate and salt to a boil. Add flour all at once and stir until a smooth ball forms. Remove from the heat; let stand for 5 minutes. Add eggs, one at a time, beating well after each addition. Continue beating until the mixture is smooth and shiny.

2. Drop by tablespoonfuls 2 in. apart onto greased baking sheets. Bake at 400° for 20-25 minutes or until set. Pierce side of each puff with tip of knife. Cool on wire racks. Split puffs open. Pull out and discard soft dough from inside tops and bottoms.

3. For the filling, in a small saucepan, combine the chocolate chips, milk and marmalade. Cook and stir until chips are melted. Cool to room temperature. Stir in orange liqueur; fold in whipped topping. Refrigerate until ready to use.

4. For the syrup, in a small saucepan, combine the sugar, cocoa, cornstarch and salt. Stir in water until blended. Bring to a boil; cook and stir mixture for 2 minutes or until thickened. Remove from the heat; stir in vanilla. Cool to room temperature.

5. Just before serving, fill the puffs with chocolate filling; drizzle with the chocolate syrup.

BAKING MORSELS

_____   _____
_____   _____
_____   _____
_____   _____
_____   _____
_____   _____

Chocolate-Orange
Cream Puffs

CHERRY CORDIAL CAKE BALLS

Brandy and coffee add mild flavor to these scrumptious cherry cake balls.

—SUSAN WESTERFIELD ALBUQUERQUE, NM

PREP: 1 HOUR • **BAKE:** 35 MIN. + STANDING
MAKES: 6 DOZEN

- 1 **package fudge marble cake mix (regular size)**
- 1¼ **cups plus 3 tablespoons strong brewed coffee, divided**
- ¼ **cup canola oil**
- 3 **large eggs**
- 1 **jar (10 ounces) maraschino cherries without stems, well drained**
- ⅓ **cup brandy**
- ¼ **cup cherry preserves**
- 1 **cup canned chocolate frosting**
- 4 **pounds milk chocolate candy coating, chopped**
- 2 **tablespoons shortening**

1. In a large bowl, combine the cake mix, 1¼ cups coffee, oil and eggs; beat on low speed for 30 seconds. Beat on medium for 2 minutes.

2. Pour batter into a greased and floured 13x9-in. baking pan. Bake at 350° for 30-35 minutes or until a toothpick inserted near the center comes out clean. Cool completely. Place the cherries in a food processor; cover and process until coarsely chopped. Transfer to a small bowl; stir in the brandy, preserves and the remaining coffee.

3. Crumble cake into a large bowl. Add frosting and cherry mixture; beat well. Shape into 1-in. balls.

4. In a microwave, melt candy coating and shortening; stir until smooth. Dip balls in chocolate mixture; allow excess to drip off. Place on waxed paper; let stand until set. Store in an airtight container overnight before serving.

CHOCOLATE CHIP PUMPKIN MUFFINS

PREP: 15 MIN. • **BAKE:** 20 MIN.
MAKES: 1 DOZEN

- 2 cups all-purpose flour
- 2½ teaspoons baking powder
- 1 teaspoon ground ginger
- 1 teaspoon ground cinnamon
- ¾ teaspoon salt
- ¼ teaspoon baking soda
  Dash ground allspice
- 1 large egg
- ¾ cup packed brown sugar
- ¾ cup canned pumpkin
- ⅔ cup milk
- 3 tablespoons butter, melted
- 1 teaspoon vanilla extract
- ½ cup miniature semisweet chocolate chips

1. In a large bowl, combine the first seven ingredients. Combine the egg, brown sugar, pumpkin, milk, butter and vanilla; stir into dry ingredients just until moistened. Stir in chocolate chips.
2. Fill greased or paper-lined muffin cups three-fourths full. Bake at 375° for 18-22 minutes or until a toothpick comes out clean. Cool for 5 minutes before removing from the pan to a wire rack.

> You can't go wrong with this recipe. It's simple, yet filling and delicious.
>
> **—JENNIFER JACKSON**
> CHARLOTTESVILLE, VA

CANDY BAR CROISSANTS

Combine convenient refrigerated crescent rolls and chocolate bars to prepare these buttery croissants. They taste as good as they look.

—BEVERLY STERLING GASPORT, NY

PREP: 15 MIN. • **BAKE:** 15 MIN. + COOLING
MAKES: 8 SERVINGS

- 1 tube (8 ounces) refrigerated crescent rolls
- 1 tablespoon butter, softened
- 2 plain milk chocolate candy bars (1.55 ounces each), broken into small pieces
- 1 large egg, lightly beaten
- 2 tablespoons sliced almonds

1. Unroll crescent roll dough; separate into triangles. Brush with the butter. Arrange candy bar pieces evenly over triangles; roll up from the wide end.
2. Place point side down on a greased baking sheet; curve ends slightly. Brush with egg and sprinkle with almonds. Bake at 375° for 11-13 minutes or until golden brown. Cool on a wire rack.

CHOCOLATE-FILLED CREAM PUFFS

This is a cherished recipe from my mother, and I'm happy to share it with others now.

—DIANA VOLAND MARTINSVILLE, IN

PREP: 40 MIN.
BAKE: 25 MIN./BATCH + COOLING
MAKES: 3 DOZEN

- 1 **cup water**
- ½ **cup butter, cubed**
- 1 **cup all-purpose flour**
- 4 **large eggs**

CHOCOLATE CREAM FILLING

- ¾ **cup sugar**
- 5 **tablespoons baking cocoa**
- 3 **tablespoons cornstarch**
- ½ **teaspoon salt**
- 2 **cups 2% milk**
- 2 **large egg yolks, lightly beaten**
- 1 **tablespoon butter**
- 1 **teaspoon vanilla extract**
  Hot fudge ice cream topping, coarse sugar, white chocolate shavings or confectioners' sugar, optional

1. In a large saucepan, bring water and butter to a boil. Add flour all at once and stir until a smooth ball forms. Remove from the heat; let stand for 5 minutes. Add eggs, one at a time, beating well after each addition. Continue beating until mixture is smooth and shiny.

2. Drop by rounded tablespoonfuls 3 in. apart onto greased baking sheets. Bake at 400° for 20-25 minutes or until golden brown. Remove to wire racks. Immediately split puffs open; remove tops and set aside. Discard soft dough from inside. Cool the puffs.

3. For filling, in a large heavy saucepan, combine the sugar, cocoa, cornstarch and salt. Stir in milk until smooth. Cook and stir over medium-high heat until thickened and bubbly. Reduce heat to low; cook and stir for 2 minutes longer.

4. Remove from the heat. Stir a small amount of hot mixture into egg yolks; return all to the pan, stirring constantly. Bring to a gentle boil; cook and stir for 2 minutes longer. Remove from the heat. Gently stir in butter and vanilla. Cover with waxed paper or plastic wrap. Cool for 15 minutes without stirring.

5. To serve, spoon chocolate cream filling into puffs; replace tops. Top with warmed hot fudge sauce, coarse sugar, white chocolate shavings or confectioners' sugar if desired.

CHOCOLATE BANANA BRAN MUFFINS

So simple to make, these treats are healthy but still satisfy my chocolate-loving family. Stir in raisin bran instead of bran flakes for a little extra flavorful touch.

—TRACY CHAPPELL HAMIOTA, MB

START TO FINISH: 25 MIN.
MAKES: 1 DOZEN

- 1 **cup all-purpose flour**
- ½ **cup sugar**
- 2 **tablespoons baking cocoa**
- 1 **teaspoon baking powder**
- 1 **teaspoon baking soda**
- ½ **teaspoon salt**
- 1 **cup bran flakes**
- 2 **large eggs**
- 1 **cup mashed ripe bananas (about 2 medium)**
- ⅓ **cup canola oil**
- ¼ **cup buttermilk**

1. Preheat oven to 400°. In a large bowl, whisk the first six ingredients. Stir in bran flakes. In another bowl, whisk eggs, bananas, oil and buttermilk until blended. Add to flour mixture; stir just until moistened.

2. Fill foil-lined muffin cups three-fourths full. Bake for 12-14 minutes or until a toothpick inserted into center comes out clean. Cool for 5 minutes before removing from pan to a wire rack. Serve warm.

Chocolate Cream
Cupcakes

CHOCOLATE CREAM CUPCAKES

My favorite hockey team, the Boston Bruins, inspired these cupcakes when they won the Stanley Cup in 2011. I like to decorate them with a "B," but you can add a love note on top using white icing.

—ALISA CHRISTENSEN
RANCHO SANTA MARGARITA, CA

PREP: 30 MIN. + CHILLING
BAKE: 20 MIN. + COOLING
MAKES: 20 CUPCAKES

- 1 **package yellow cake mix (regular size)**
- 1 **package (3.4 ounces) cook-and-serve chocolate pudding mix**

GLAZE

- ⅔ **cup semisweet chocolate chips**
- 2½ **tablespoons butter**
- 1¼ **cups confectioners' sugar**
- 3 **tablespoons hot water**
  White decorating icing, optional

1. Prepare cake mix according to package directions for cupcakes, using 20 paper-lined muffin cups. Cool for 10 minutes; remove to wire racks.

2. Meanwhile, in a small bowl, prepare pudding mix according to the package directions. Press plastic wrap onto the surface of pudding; refrigerate until cold.

3. Cut a small hole in the tip of a pastry bag or in a corner of a food-safe plastic bag; insert a small pastry tip. Transfer pudding to bag. Using a wooden or metal skewer, poke a hole through bottom of cupcake liners. Push tip through hole and pipe filling into cupcakes.

4. In a microwave, melt the chocolate chips and butter; stir until smooth. Whisk in confectioners' sugar and water. Dip tops of cupcakes into glaze. If desired, pipe designs on cupcakes.

PEPPERMINT PUFF PASTRY STICKS

I wanted to impress my husband's family with something you might expect to find in a European bakery. The chocolaty sticks I created are surprisingly easy to fix using frozen puff pastry.

—DARLENE BRENDEN SALEM, OR

PREP: 15 MIN.
BAKE: 15 MIN./BATCH + COOLING
MAKES: ABOUT 3 DOZEN

- 1 **sheet frozen puff pastry, thawed**
- 1½ **cups crushed peppermint candies**
- 10 **ounces milk chocolate candy coating, coarsely chopped**

1. Preheat oven to 400°. Unfold the pastry sheet. Cut in half to form two rectangles. Cut each rectangle crosswise into 18 strips, about ½ in. wide. Place on ungreased baking sheets. Bake 12-15 minutes or until golden brown. Remove from pans to wire racks to cool completely.

2. Place crushed candies in a shallow bowl. In a microwave, melt the candy coating; stir until smooth. Dip each cookie halfway in coating; allow excess to drip off. Sprinkle with peppermint candies. Place on waxed paper; let stand until set. Store cookies in an airtight container.

CHOCOLATE ECLAIRS

PREP: 45 MIN.
BAKE: 35 MIN. + COOLING
MAKES: 9 SERVINGS

- **1 cup water**
- **½ cup butter, cubed**
- **¼ teaspoon salt**
- **1 cup all-purpose flour**
- **4 large eggs**

FILLING
- **2½ cups cold milk**
- **1 package (5.1 ounces) instant vanilla pudding mix**
- **1 cup heavy whipping cream**
- **¼ cup confectioners' sugar**
- **1 teaspoon vanilla extract**

FROSTING
- **2 ounces semisweet chocolate**
- **2 tablespoons butter**
- **1¼ cups confectioners' sugar**
- **2 to 3 tablespoons hot water**

1. Preheat oven to 400°. In a large saucepan, bring water, butter and salt to a boil. Add flour all at once and stir until a smooth ball forms. Remove from heat; let stand 5 minutes. Add the eggs, one at a time, beating well after each addition. Continue beating until mixture is smooth and shiny.

2. Using a tablespoon or a pastry tube with a #10 or large tip, form dough into 4x1½-in. strips on a greased baking sheet. Bake for 35-40 minutes or until puffed and golden. Remove to a wire rack. Immediately split eclairs open; remove tops and set aside. Discard soft dough from inside. Cool eclairs.

3. In a large bowl, beat the milk and pudding mix according to package directions. In another bowl, whip the cream until soft peaks form. Beat in sugar and vanilla; fold into pudding. Fill eclairs (chill any remaining filling for another use).

4. For the frosting, in a microwave, melt the chocolate and butter; stir until smooth. Stir in sugar and enough hot water to achieve a smooth consistency. Cool slightly. Frost the eclairs. Store in refrigerator.

Homemade eclairs, with their creamy filling and fudgy frosting, will definitely stand out at a special occasion. Family and friends will ooh and aah over these.

—JESSICA CAMPBELL VIOLA, WI

CHOCOLATE ANGEL CUPCAKES WITH COCONUT CREAM FROSTING

Sweeten any meal with these fun frosted chocolate cupcakes that take just minutes to prepare. Better yet, the finger-licking-good taste packs far fewer calories and fat than traditional desserts.

—**MANDY RIVERS** LEXINGTON, SC

PREP: 15 MIN. • **BAKE:** 15 MIN. + COOLING
MAKES: 2 DOZEN

- 1 **package (16 ounces) angel food cake mix**
- ¾ **cup baking cocoa**
- 1 **cup (8 ounces) reduced-fat sour cream**
- 1 **cup confectioners' sugar**
- ⅛ **teaspoon coconut extract**
- 2½ **cups reduced-fat whipped topping**
- ¾ **cup flaked coconut, toasted**

1. Prepare the cake mix according to package directions for cupcakes, adding cocoa when mixing.
2. Fill foil- or paper-lined muffin cups two-thirds full. Bake at 375° for 11-15 minutes or until the cake springs back when lightly touched and cracks feel dry. Cool for 10 minutes before removing from pans to wire racks to cool completely.
3. For the frosting, in a large bowl, combine sour cream, confectioners' sugar and extract until smooth. Fold in whipped topping. Frost cupcakes. Sprinkle with the toasted coconut. Refrigerate leftovers.

Peanut Butter
Chocolate Cupcakes

PEANUT BUTTER CHOCOLATE CUPCAKES

PREP: 30 MIN. • **BAKE:** 25 MIN. + COOLING
MAKES: 1 DOZEN JUMBO CUPCAKES

- 1 **package (3 ounces) cream cheese, softened**
- ¼ **cup creamy peanut butter**
- 2 **tablespoons sugar**
- 1 **tablespoon 2% milk**

BATTER
- 2 **cups sugar**
- 1¾ **cups all-purpose flour**
- ½ **cup baking cocoa**
- 1½ **teaspoons baking powder**
- 1 **teaspoon salt**
- ¼ **teaspoon baking soda**
- 2 **large eggs**
- 1 **cup water**
- 1 **cup 2% milk**
- ½ **cup canola oil**
- 2 **teaspoons vanilla extract**

FROSTING
- ⅓ **cup butter, softened**
- 2 **cups confectioners' sugar**
- 6 **tablespoons baking cocoa**
- 3 **to 4 tablespoons 2% milk**

1. In a small bowl, beat cream cheese, peanut butter, sugar and milk until smooth; set aside.

2. In a large bowl, combine the sugar, flour, cocoa, baking powder, salt and baking soda. In another bowl, whisk the eggs, water, milk, oil and vanilla. Stir into the dry ingredients just until moistened (batter will be thin).

3. Fill paper-lined jumbo muffin cups half full with batter. Drop a scant tablespoonful of peanut butter mixture into the center of each; cover with remaining batter.

4. Bake at 350° for 25-30 minutes or until a toothpick inserted into cake comes out clean. Cool for 10 minutes; remove cupcakes from pans to wire racks. Cool completely.

5. In a large bowl, combine frosting ingredients until smooth; frost the cupcakes. Store in the refrigerator.

> I can't get enough of chocolate and peanut butter together, but I didn't have any luck finding a peanut butter-filled chocolate cupcake recipe. Instead, I experimented with my go-to chocolate cupcake recipe and made a filling I loved.
>
> **—JULIE SMALL** UNITY, NH

BAKING MORSELS

_____   _____
_____   _____
_____   _____
_____   _____

BAKED LONG JOHNS

Because you don't have to fry these doughnuts, you can feel especially good about having them for breakfast!

—NICKI LAZORIK MELLEN, WI

PREP: 15 MIN. • **BAKE:** 20 MIN. + COOLING
MAKES: 8 SERVINGS

- 2 **cups all-purpose flour**
- ½ **cup sugar**
- 2 **teaspoons baking powder**
- ½ **teaspoon salt**
- ¼ **teaspoon ground cinnamon**
- 2 **large eggs**
- ¾ **cup fat-free milk**
- 1 **tablespoon butter, melted**
- 1 **teaspoon vanilla extract**

GLAZE
- ¾ **cup semisweet chocolate chips**
- 1 **tablespoon butter**
- 4½ **teaspoons fat-free milk**

1. In a small bowl, combine the flour, sugar, baking powder, salt and cinnamon. In another bowl, whisk the eggs, milk, butter and vanilla. Stir into dry ingredients just until moistened.

2. Transfer to eight 4½x2½x1½-in. loaf pans coated with cooking spray. Bake at 325° for 18-22 minutes or until golden brown. Immediately remove doughnuts from pans to a wire rack to cool completely.

3. In a microwave, melt chocolate chips and butter. Add milk; stir until smooth. Dip the tops of doughnuts into glaze. Return to wire rack; let stand until set.

CREAM-FILLED CHOCOLATE SUPREME MUFFINS

My mom had a reputation for baking up delicious things, and she used to sell muffins at my dad's workplace. These cupcake-like treats were always a hit.

—SUSANNE SPICKER NORTH OGDEN, UT

PREP: 30 MIN.
BAKE: 25 MIN. + COOLING
MAKES: 1 DOZEN

- 3 cups all-purpose flour
- 2 cups sugar
- ½ cup baking cocoa
- 2 teaspoons baking soda
- 1 teaspoon salt
- 2 cups cold water
- ¾ cup canola oil
- 1 large egg
- 2 tablespoons white vinegar
- 2 teaspoons vanilla extract

FILLING
- 4 ounces cream cheese, softened
- ¼ cup sugar
- ⅛ teaspoon salt
- 2 tablespoons beaten egg
- ½ teaspoon vanilla extract
- ¾ cup milk chocolate chips
  Confectioners' sugar, optional

1. Preheat oven to 350°. In a large bowl, combine the flour, sugar, cocoa, baking soda and salt. In another bowl, combine the water, oil, egg, vinegar and vanilla. Stir into dry ingredients just until moistened.

2. For filling, beat cream cheese, sugar and salt until smooth. Beat in egg and vanilla. Fold in chips.

3. Fill 12 paper-lined jumbo muffin cups half full with batter. Drop a rounded tablespoonful of the cream cheese mixture into center of each; cover with remaining batter.

4. Bake for 25-30 minutes or until a toothpick inserted into muffin comes out clean. Cool 5 minutes before removing from pans to wire racks to cool completely. Sprinkle muffins with confectioners' sugar if desired.

NUTTY CHOCOLATE MUFFINS

Mixing in chopped peanuts sets these muffins apart from others. I'll often serve these at Christmastime, but they're popular any time of year.
—**MARY LISA SPEER** PALM BEACH, FL

PREP: 30 MIN. • **BAKE:** 25 MIN. + COOLING
MAKES: 16 SERVINGS

- 1¾ cups all-purpose flour
- 1¼ cups plus 2 tablespoons packed brown sugar
- ⅔ cup baking cocoa
- 1 teaspoon baking soda
- 1 teaspoon baking powder
- ½ teaspoon salt
- 2 large eggs
- 1 cup buttermilk
- ½ cup butter, melted
- 2½ teaspoons vanilla extract
- 1 cup chopped unsalted peanuts
- 1 cup semisweet chocolate chips

FILLING
- 1 cup creamy peanut butter
- 3 tablespoons butter, softened
- ¾ cup confectioners' sugar
- ¼ teaspoon vanilla extract

1. In a large bowl, combine first six ingredients. In another bowl, whisk eggs, buttermilk, butter and vanilla. Stir into dry ingredients just until moistened. Fold in peanuts and chocolate chips. Fill paper-lined muffin cups two-thirds full.

2. Bake at 350° for 22-25 minutes or until a toothpick inserted near the center comes out clean. Cool for 10 minutes before removing from pans to wire racks to cool completely.

3. In a small bowl, beat the peanut butter, butter, confectioners' sugar and vanilla until fluffy. Cut a small hole in the corner of a pastry or plastic bag; insert a large star tip. Fill bag with peanut butter filling. Insert tip into the top of each cupcake; fill with about 2 teaspoons filling, gradually lifting tip and piping a small amount of filling onto muffin tops. Refrigerate leftovers.

Nutty Chocolate
Muffins

Marbled Cappuccino
Fudge Cheesecake

Chocolate
Desserts

MARBLED CAPPUCCINO FUDGE CHEESECAKE

PREP: 45 MIN.
BAKE: 70 MIN. + CHILLING
MAKES: 12 SERVINGS

- 1½ **cups chocolate graham cracker crumbs (about 8 whole crackers)**
- 3 **tablespoons sugar**
- ¼ **cup butter, melted**

FILLING

- 4 **packages (8 ounces each) cream cheese, softened**
- 1¼ **cups sugar**
- ¼ **cup heavy whipping cream**
- 3 **tablespoons double mocha cappuccino mix**
- 2 **tablespoons all-purpose flour**
- 1½ **teaspoons vanilla extract**
- 3 **large eggs, lightly beaten**
- ⅔ **cup hot fudge ice cream topping, warmed**

CAPPUCCINO CREAM TOPPING

- 1 **cup heavy whipping cream**
- 2 **tablespoons double mocha cappuccino mix**
- 1 **tablespoon confectioners' sugar**
  Chocolate curls, optional

1. Place a greased 9-in. springform pan on a double thickness of heavy-duty foil (about 18 in. square). Securely wrap foil around pan.

2. In a small bowl, combine the cracker crumbs, sugar and butter. Press onto the bottom and 2 in. up the sides of prepared pan. Place pan on a baking sheet. Bake at 325° for 7-9 minutes. Cool on a wire rack.

3. In a large bowl, beat cream cheese and sugar until smooth. Beat in the cream, cappuccino mix, flour and vanilla. Add eggs; beat on low speed just until combined. Pour half of batter into crust. Drizzle with ⅓ cup fudge topping. Repeat layers. Cut through the batter with a knife to swirl fudge topping. Place springform pan in a large baking pan; add 1 in. of hot water to larger pan.

4. Bake at 325° for 70-80 minutes or until center is just set and top appears dull. Remove springform pan from the water bath. Cool on a wire rack for 10 minutes. Carefully run a knife around the edge of pan to loosen; cool 1 hour longer. Refrigerate overnight. Remove sides of pan.

5. For topping, in a small bowl, beat cream until it begins to thicken. Add the cappuccino mix and confectioners' sugar; beat until soft peaks form. Spread the topping over cheesecake. Garnish with chocolate curls if desired.

> I love the frozen cappuccino drinks at coffee shops and wanted a cheesecake with the same goodness. If you try it, don't hold back on the cream topping. It's the best part!
>
> **—BECKY MCCLAFLIN** BLANCHARD, OK

HOT COCOA SOUFFLE

A friend invited me to go to a church cooking demo years ago, and one of the recipes prepared was this luscious souffle. It's decadently good.

—JOAN HALLFORD

NORTH RICHLAND HILLS, TX

PREP: 20 MIN. • **BAKE:** 40 MIN.
MAKES: 6 SERVINGS

- 5 **large eggs**
- 4 **teaspoons plus ¾ cup sugar, divided**
- ½ **cup baking cocoa**
- 6 **tablespoons all-purpose flour**
- ¼ **teaspoon salt**
- 1½ **cups fat-free milk**
- 2 **tablespoons butter**
- 1½ **teaspoons vanilla extract**

1. Separate eggs; let stand at room temperature for 30 minutes. Coat a 2-qt. souffle dish with cooking spray and lightly sprinkle with 4 teaspoons sugar; set aside.

2. In a small saucepan, combine the cocoa, flour, salt and remaining sugar. Gradually whisk in milk. Bring to a boil, stirring constantly. Cook and stir 1-2 minutes longer or until thickened. Stir in butter. Transfer to a large bowl.

3. Stir a small amount of hot mixture into egg yolks; return all to the bowl, stirring constantly. Add the vanilla; cool slightly.

4. In another large bowl, with clean beaters, beat egg whites until stiff peaks form. With a spatula, stir a fourth of the egg whites into chocolate mixture until no white streaks remain. Fold in the remaining egg whites until combined.

5. Transfer to prepared dish. Bake at 350° for 40-45 minutes or until the top is puffed and the center appears set. Serve immediately.

PEANUT BUTTER CHOCOLATE DESSERT

For me, the ideal dessert combines chocolate and peanut butter. This is a cinch to whip together because it doesn't require any baking.
—DEBBIE PRICE LARUE, OH

PREP: 20 MIN. + CHILLING
MAKES: 12-16 SERVINGS

- 20 **chocolate cream-filled chocolate sandwich cookies, divided**
- 2 **tablespoons butter, softened**
- 1 **package (8 ounces) cream cheese, softened**
- ½ **cup peanut butter**
- 1½ **cups confectioners' sugar, divided**
- 1 **carton (16 ounces) frozen whipped topping, thawed, divided**
- 15 **miniature peanut butter cups, chopped**
- 1 **cup cold milk**
- 1 **package (3.9 ounces) instant chocolate fudge pudding mix**

1. Crush 16 cookies; toss with the butter. Press into an ungreased 9-in. square dish; set aside.

2. In a large bowl, beat the cream cheese, peanut butter and 1 cup of confectioners' sugar until smooth. Fold in half of the whipped topping. Spread over the crust. Sprinkle with peanut butter cups.

3. In another large bowl, beat the milk, pudding mix and remaining confectioners' sugar on low speed for 2 minutes. Let stand for 2 minutes or until soft-set. Fold in the remaining whipped topping.

4. Spread over the peanut butter cups. Crush the remaining cookies; sprinkle over the top. Cover and chill for at least 3 hours.

BAKING MORSELS

SIMPLE TURTLE CHEESECAKE

For an almost instant dessert, I spread homemade ganache and caramel sauce over premade cheesecake. It makes party hosting a little less hectic.

—LAURA MCDOWELL LAKE VILLA, IL

START TO FINISH: 25 MIN.
MAKES: 8 SERVINGS

- 1 **frozen New York-style cheesecake (30 ounces), thawed**
- ½ **cup semisweet chocolate chips**
- ½ **cup heavy whipping cream, divided**
- 3 **tablespoons chopped pecans, toasted**
- ¼ **cup butter, cubed**
- ½ **cup plus 2 tablespoons packed brown sugar**
- 1 **tablespoon light corn syrup**

1. Place cheesecake on a serving plate. Place chocolate chips in a small bowl. In a small saucepan, bring ¼ cup cream just to a boil. Pour over chocolate; stir with a whisk until smooth. Cool slightly, stirring occasionally. Pour over cheesecake; sprinkle with the pecans. Refrigerate until set.

2. In a small saucepan, melt butter; stir in the brown sugar and corn syrup. Bring to a boil. Reduce heat; cook and stir until the sugar is dissolved. Stir in the remaining cream and return to a boil. Remove from the heat. Serve sauce warm with cheesecake or, if desired, cool completely and drizzle over cheesecake.

NOTE *To toast nuts, bake in a shallow pan in a 350° oven for 5-10 minutes or cook in a skillet over low heat until lightly browned, stirring occasionally.*

WHEN TO CHOP NUTS

If the word "chopped" comes before the ingredient when listed in a recipe (such as the pecans in Simple Turtle Cheesecake), then chop the ingredient before measuring. If the word "chopped" comes after, then chop after measuring.

Simple Turtle
Cheesecake

S'MORES-DIPPED APPLES

I don't think you can beat chocolate, marshmallows, graham crackers and apples together in a snack. Whenever I take these to a bake sale, they sell out in a flash.

—MARIA REGAKIS SAUGUS, MA

PREP: 20 MIN.
COOK: 10 MIN. + CHILLING
MAKES: 8 SERVINGS

- 8 large Granny Smith apples
- 8 wooden pop sticks
- 2 tablespoons butter
- 2 packages (16 ounces each) large marshmallows
- 2 cups coarsely crushed graham crackers
- 1 package (11½ ounces) milk chocolate chips

1. Line a baking sheet with waxed paper; generously coat waxed paper with cooking spray. Wash and dry apples; remove stems. Insert pop sticks into apples.

2. In a large heavy saucepan, melt the butter over medium heat. Add the marshmallows; stir until melted. Dip the apples, one at a time, into warm marshmallow mixture, allowing excess to drip off. Place on prepared baking sheet and refrigerate until set, about 15 minutes.

3. Place graham cracker crumbs in a shallow dish. In top of a double boiler or a metal bowl over barely simmering water, melt chocolate chips; stir until smooth. Dip bottom half of apples into chocolate, then into cracker crumbs. Place on baking sheet. Refrigerate until set.

HAZELNUT CHOCOLATE MOUSSE

If you really love chocolate, you can turn this mousse into the ultimate chocolaty dessert dream. I sometimes use a chocolate fudge-flavored pudding mix or chocolate-flavored Cool Whip instead of regular Cool Whip.

—KARLA KROHN MADISON, WI

START TO FINISH: 10 MIN.
MAKES: 6 SERVINGS

- 1¾ cups cold 2% milk
- 1 package (3.9 ounces) instant chocolate pudding mix
- ½ cup Nutella
- 1¾ cups whipped topping
    Additional whipped topping

1. Whisk milk and pudding mix in a large bowl for 2 minutes. Let stand for 2 minutes or until soft-set. Whisk in Nutella until smooth. Fold in the whipped topping.

2. Spoon into six dessert dishes. Chill until serving. Garnish servings with additional whipped topping.

CARAMEL FUDGE CHEESECAKE

I combined several recipes to satisfy both the chocolate enthusiasts and cheesecake fans in my family. With a fudge brownie crust, crunchy pecans and a gooey layer of caramel, this delight is hard to resist.

—BRENDA RUSE TRURO, NS

PREP: 30 MIN. • **BAKE:** 35 MIN. + CHILLING
MAKES: 12 SERVINGS

- 1 **package fudge brownie mix (8-inch square pan size)**
- 1 **package (14 ounces) caramels**
- ¼ **cup evaporated milk**
- 1¼ **cups coarsely chopped pecans**
- 2 **packages (8 ounces each) cream cheese, softened**
- ½ **cup sugar**
- 2 **large eggs, lightly beaten**
- 2 **ounces unsweetened chocolate, melted and cooled**
  Chocolate curls, optional

1. Prepare brownie batter according to package directions. Spread into a greased 9-in. springform pan. Place pan on a baking sheet. Bake at 350° for 20 minutes. Place pan on a wire rack for 10 minutes (leave oven on).

2. Meanwhile, in a microwave-safe bowl, melt the caramels with milk. Pour over the brownie crust; sprinkle with pecans.

3. In a large bowl, beat cream cheese and sugar until light and fluffy. Add the eggs; beat on low speed just until combined. Stir in the melted chocolate. Pour over the pecans. Return pan to baking sheet.

4. Bake for 35-40 minutes or until the center is almost set. Cool on a wire rack for 10 minutes. Run a knife around the edge of pan to loosen; cool 1 hour longer. Refrigerate overnight. Remove sides of pan. Garnish cake with chocolate curls if desired.

Black Forest
Cannoli Parfaits

BLACK FOREST CANNOLI PARFAITS

My family loves cannoli, but making the shells can be a bit tedious. These parfaits are an easy way to enjoy the flavor without spending time baking the shells.

—**ANNA GINSBERG** AUSTIN, TX

PREP: 25 MIN. + CHILLING
MAKES: 8 SERVINGS

- 1 **package (16 ounces) frozen pitted tart cherries, thawed**
- 2 **tablespoons sugar**
- 1 **tablespoon cornstarch**
- 2 **teaspoons lemon juice**

PARFAIT

- 1 **carton (15 ounces) reduced-fat ricotta cheese**
- 1 **package (8 ounces) fat-free cream cheese**
- ¼ **cup sugar**
- 2 **tablespoons maple syrup**
- 2 **teaspoons lemon juice**
- 2 **teaspoons vanilla extract**
- 2 **cups reduced-fat whipped topping**
- ⅓ **cup miniature semisweet chocolate chips**
- 20 **chocolate wafers, crushed**

1. Drain cherries, reserving liquid in a 1-cup measuring cup. Add enough water to measure ⅓ cup; set aside.

2. In a small saucepan, combine the sugar and cornstarch; stir in reserved cherry juice mixture until smooth. Bring to a boil; cook and stir for 2 minutes or until thickened. Remove from the heat; stir in cherries and lemon juice. Cool.

3. Place the ricotta, cream cheese and sugar in a food processor; cover and process until smooth. Add the syrup, lemon juice and vanilla; process until combined. Gently fold in whipped topping and chocolate chips.

4. Place 1 tablespoon crushed wafers in each of eight parfait glasses. Top with ⅓ cup cheese mixture and a heaping tablespoonful of cherry sauce. Repeat layers. Refrigerate for at least 2 hours before serving.

BAKING MORSELS

PEANUT BUTTER PARFAITS

If you're looking for a super dessert that can be made a day ahead, give this a try. Just pull it out of the refrigerator when it's snack time or when the guests arrive. Yum!

—MARY ANN LEE CLIFTON PARK, NY

PREP: 40 MIN. • **COOK:** 10 MIN.
MAKES: 6 SERVINGS

- 1½ teaspoons unflavored gelatin
- 2 tablespoons cold water
- 1 cup 2% milk
- ¼ cup sugar
- ¼ cup creamy peanut butter
- 2 tablespoons butter
- 2 large egg yolks, beaten
- 1 teaspoon vanilla extract
- 1 cup heavy whipping cream
- 3 tablespoons confectioners' sugar
- ¾ cup hot fudge ice cream topping
- 3 tablespoons chopped salted peanuts
  Chocolate curls

1. Sprinkle gelatin over cold water; let stand for 1 minute. Microwave on high for 20 seconds. Stir and let stand for 1 minute or until gelatin is dissolved.

2. In a small heavy saucepan, heat the milk, sugar, peanut butter and butter until bubbles form around sides of pan. Whisk a small amount of hot mixture into the egg yolks. Return all to the pan, whisking constantly.

3. Cook and stir over low heat until the mixture is thickened and coats the back of a spoon. Stir in gelatin mixture and vanilla. Quickly transfer to a bowl; place in ice water and stir mixture for 10 minutes or until cold and thickened.

4. In a large bowl, beat cream until it begins to thicken. Add confectioners' sugar; beat until soft peaks form. Fold half into peanut butter mixture.

5. Spoon 1 tablespoon of hot fudge topping into each of six parfait glasses. Top with ¼ cup of peanut butter mixture. Repeat layers. Top with the remaining whipped cream; sprinkle with peanuts and chocolate curls. Chill until serving.

SPECIAL PARFAITS

Want to add a sweet touch to your parfait glasses? Melt chocolate chips and shortening in a microwave-safe bowl; stir until smooth. Dip rims of parfait glasses into the melted chocolate, then sprinkle chocolate jimmies over rims. Stand glasses upright; set aside until chocolate hardens.

IRISH CREME CHOCOLATE TRIFLE

I created this trifle when I was given a bottle of Irish cream liqueur as a gift and had leftover peppermint candy. I've also made it with Irish creme coffee creamer and replaced the mint candies with beautiful chocolate curls.

—**MARGARET WILSON** SUN CITY, CA

PREP: 20 MIN. • **BAKE:** 30 MIN. + CHILLING
MAKES: 16 SERVINGS

- 1 **package devil's food cake mix (regular size)**
- 1 **cup refrigerated Irish creme nondairy creamer**
- 3½ **cups cold milk**
- 2 **packages (3.9 ounces each) instant chocolate pudding mix**
- 3 **cups whipped topping**
- 12 **mint candies, chopped**

1. Prepare and bake cake according to package directions, using a greased 13x9-in. baking pan. Cool on a wire rack for 1 hour.

2. With a meat fork or wooden skewer, carefully poke holes in cake about 2 in. apart. Slowly pour creamer over cake; refrigerate for 1 hour.

3. In a large bowl, whisk the milk and pudding mixes for 2 minutes. Let stand for 2 minutes or until soft-set.

4. Cut cake into 1½-in. cubes; place a third of the cubes in a 3-qt. glass bowl. Top with a third of the pudding, whipped topping and candies; repeat layers twice. Store in the refrigerator.

Marshmallow
Monkey Business

MARSHMALLOW MONKEY BUSINESS

Just like kids, I love fun treats! These pops are doubly good because they are so simple to make and package—just wrap them in cellophane bags.

—SUSAN SCARBOROUGH

FERNANDINA BEACH, FL

PREP: 30 MIN. • **COOK:** 10 MIN.
MAKES: 20 SERVINGS

- 1 **package (10 ounces) large marshmallows**
- 3 **tablespoons butter**
- 6 **cups Rice Krispies**
- ½ **cup chopped dried banana chips**
- 20 **wooden pop sticks**

TOPPING

- 2 **cups (12 ounces) semisweet chocolate chips**
- 2 **tablespoons shortening**
- ½ **cup chopped salted peanuts**
- ½ **cup chopped dried banana chips**

1. In a large saucepan, heat the marshmallows and butter until melted. Remove from the heat. Stir in the cereal and banana chips; mix well. Cool for 3 minutes.

2. Transfer mixture to waxed paper; divide into 20 portions. With buttered hands, shape each portion around a wooden pop stick to resemble a small banana.

3. In a microwave, melt the chocolate chips and shortening; stir mixture until smooth. Dip ends of "bananas" in chocolate; allow excess to drip off. Sprinkle with the peanuts and banana chips. Place on waxed paper; let stand until set. Store in an airtight container.

3D CHOCOLATE CHEESECAKE

PREP: 30 MIN.
BAKE: 55 MIN. + CHILLING
MAKES: 16 SERVINGS

- 1 **cup chocolate graham cracker crumbs (about 5 whole crackers)**
- 1 **tablespoon sugar**
- ¼ **cup butter, melted**

FILLING

- 4 **packages (8 ounces each) cream cheese, softened**
- 1⅓ **cups sugar**
- 1 **package (10 ounces) 60% cacao bittersweet chocolate baking chips, melted and cooled**
- ¼ **cup baking cocoa**
- 4 **large eggs, lightly beaten**

GANACHE

- ⅔ **cup (4 ounces) 60% cacao bittersweet chocolate baking chips**
- ½ **cup heavy whipping cream**
- 1 **tablespoon sugar**

1. Preheat oven to 325°. Place a greased 9-in. springform pan on a double thickness of heavy-duty foil (about 18 in. square). Securely wrap foil around pan.

2. In a small bowl, combine cracker crumbs and sugar; stir in butter. Press onto the bottom of prepared pan. Place pan on a baking sheet. Bake 10 minutes. Cool on a wire rack.

3. In a large bowl, beat cream cheese and sugar until smooth. Beat in cooled chocolate and cocoa. Add eggs; beat on low speed just until combined. Pour over crust. Place springform pan in a large baking pan; add 1 in. of boiling water to larger pan.

4. Bake 55-60 minutes or until center is just set and top appears dull. Remove springform pan from the water bath; remove foil. Cool cheesecake on a wire rack 10 minutes; loosen edges from pan with a knife. Cool 1 hour longer. Refrigerate overnight.

5. For ganache, place chocolate in a small bowl. In a small saucepan, bring cream and sugar just to a boil. Pour over chocolate; whisk until smooth. Cool to reach a spreading consistency, stirring occasionally.

6. Remove rim from pan. Spread ganache over cheesecake to within 1 in. of edge. Refrigerate 1 hour or until set.

> A cheesecake that is deep, dark and decadent earns the right to be called "3D." This version always looks its chocolaty best because the ganache coating hides any cracks that may have formed on the top.
>
> **—VANASSA HICKS** FLINT, MI

CHOCOLATE CHIP COOKIE DELIGHT

This recipe puts a unique spin on ordinary chocolate chip bars. Bring the dessert to your next potluck—the pan always comes home empty!

—**DIANE WINDLEY** GRACE, ID

PREP: 35 MIN. + CHILLING
MAKES: 15 SERVINGS

- 1 **tube (16½ ounces) refrigerated chocolate chip cookie dough**
- 1 **package (8 ounces) cream cheese, softened**
- 1 **cup confectioners' sugar**
- 1 **carton (12 ounces) frozen whipped topping, thawed, divided**
- 3 **cups cold 2% milk**
- 1 **package (3.9 ounces) instant chocolate pudding mix**
- 1 **package (3.4 ounces) instant vanilla pudding mix**
  Chopped nuts and chocolate curls, optional

1. Let cookie dough stand at room temperature for 5-10 minutes to soften. Press dough into an ungreased 13x9-in. baking pan. Bake at 350° for 14-16 minutes or until golden brown. Cool on a wire rack.

2. In a large bowl, beat cream cheese and confectioners' sugar until smooth. Fold in 1¾ cups whipped topping. Spread over crust.

3. In a large bowl, whisk the milk and pudding mixes for 2 minutes. Spread over cream cheese layer. Top with the remaining whipped topping. Sprinkle with nuts and chocolate curls if desired.

4. Cover and refrigerate for 8 hours or overnight until firm.

CHOCOLATE-COFFEE BEAN ICE CREAM CAKE

We celebrate faculty birthdays at our school. I needed a quick recipe that would be appealing to everyone. This tall, impressive dessert certainly fit my needs and was a huge hit.

—KAREN BECK ALEXANDRIA, PA

PREP: 15 MIN. + FREEZING
MAKES: 12 SERVINGS

1¾ **cups chocolate wafer crumbs (about 28 wafers)**
¼ **cup butter, melted**
2 **quarts coffee ice cream, softened**
⅓ **cup chocolate-covered coffee beans, finely chopped**
2¼ **cups heavy whipping cream**
1 **cup plus 2 tablespoons confectioners' sugar**
½ **cup plus 1 tablespoon baking cocoa**
½ **teaspoon vanilla extract**
Chocolate curls and additional chocolate-covered coffee beans

1. In a small bowl, combine the wafer crumbs and butter; press onto the bottom and up the sides of a greased 9-in. springform pan. Freeze for 10 minutes.

2. In a large bowl, combine the ice cream and coffee beans; spoon over crust. Cover and freeze for 2 hours or until firm.

3. In a large bowl, beat cream until it begins to thicken. Add confectioners' sugar, cocoa and vanilla; beat until stiff peaks form. Spread over ice cream. (Pan will be full.)

4. Cover and freeze for 4 hours or overnight. Remove from the freezer 10 minutes before serving. Garnish with chocolate curls and coffee beans.

CHOCOLATE ALMOND ICE CREAM

It wouldn't be summer for our family without this cool treat. Even though electric ice cream makers are available, I still prefer to hand-crank ice cream.

—ALICE HICKEN HEBER CITY, UT

PREP: 30 MIN. + CHILLING
PROCESS: 20 MIN./BATCH + FREEZING
MAKES: 2½ QUARTS

- 2 **envelopes unflavored gelatin**
- 6 **tablespoons cold water**
- 3 **cups milk**
- 3 **cups sugar**
- ¼ **teaspoon salt**
- 3 **large eggs, lightly beaten**
- 6 **to 7 ounces unsweetened chocolate, melted**
- 4 **cups heavy whipping cream**
- 2 **teaspoons vanilla extract**
- 1 **cup sliced or slivered almonds, toasted**

1. In a small bowl, sprinkle gelatin over cold water; let stand for at least 2 minutes. In a large heavy saucepan, heat the milk, sugar and salt until bubbles form around sides of the pan. Whisk a small amount of hot mixture into the eggs. Return all to the pan, whisking constantly.

2. Cook and stir over low heat until mixture is thickened and coats the back of a spoon. Remove from the heat. Stir in gelatin mixture until dissolved; stir in chocolate until blended. Cool quickly by placing pan in a bowl of ice water; stir for 2 minutes. Stir in cream and vanilla. Press plastic wrap onto surface of custard. Refrigerate for several hours or overnight.

3. Fill cylinder of ice cream freezer two-thirds full; freeze according to manufacturer's directions. Refrigerate the remaining mixture until ready to freeze. When ice cream is frozen, stir in almonds. Transfer to a freezer container; freeze for 2-4 hours before serving ice cream.

ROCKY ROAD GRILLED BANANA SPLITS

There's no wrong turn when you travel down this rocky road! Toasty-warm bananas filled with gooey goodness and topped with heaping scoops of creamy perfection are a new cookout must-have.

—LORETTA OUELLETTE POMPANO BEACH, FL

START TO FINISH: 20 MIN.
MAKES: 4 SERVINGS

- 4 **medium firm bananas, unpeeled**
- 1 **dark chocolate candy bar with almonds (3½ ounces)**
- ¾ **cup miniature marshmallows, divided**
- 1 **quart rocky road ice cream**
   Whipped cream in a can

1. Place each banana on a 12-in. square of foil; crimp and shape the foil around bananas so they sit flat.

2. Cut each banana lengthwise about ½ in. deep, leaving ½ in. uncut at both ends. Gently pull each banana peel open, forming a pocket. Finely chop half of the candy bar. Fill pockets with chopped chocolate and ½ cup marshmallows.

3. Grill the bananas, covered, over medium heat for 8-10 minutes or until marshmallows are melted and golden brown. Transfer each banana to a serving plate; top with scoops of ice cream. Break remaining chocolate into pieces. Sprinkle chocolate pieces and remaining marshmallows over tops. Garnish with whipped cream.

CHOCOLATE TRIFLE

For a fabulous finale when entertaining, this lovely layered trifle is a winner! It's a make-ahead dessert that serves a group, and even tastes great the next day.
—**PAM BOTINE** GOLDSBORO, NC

PREP: 30 MIN. + CHILLING
MAKES: 8-10 SERVINGS

- 1 **package chocolate fudge cake mix (regular size)**
- 1 **package (6 ounces) instant chocolate pudding mix**
- ½ **cup strong coffee**
- 1 **carton (12 ounces) frozen whipped topping, thawed**
- 6 **Heath candy bars (1.4 ounces each), crushed**

1. Bake cake according to package directions. Cool. Prepare the pudding according to package directions; set aside.

2. Crumble cake; reserve ½ cup. Place half of the remaining cake crumbs in the bottom of a 4½- or 5-qt. trifle dish or decorative glass bowl.

3. Layer with half of the coffee, half of the pudding, half of the whipped topping and half of the crushed candy bars. Repeat the layers of cake, coffee, pudding and whipped topping.

4. Combine the remaining crushed candy bars with reserved cake crumbs; sprinkle over the top. Refrigerate for 4-5 hours before serving.

WARM CHOCOLATE MELTING CUPS

Described as over-the-top delicious, these desserts are surprisingly smooth. But what's even more surprising is that each one has fewer than 200 calories and only 6 grams of fat.

—KISSA VAUGHN TROY, TX

PREP: 20 MIN. • **BAKE:** 20 MIN.
MAKES: 10 SERVINGS

- 1¼ **cups sugar, divided**
- ½ **cup baking cocoa**
- 2 **tablespoons all-purpose flour**
- ⅛ **teaspoon salt**
- ¾ **cup water**
- ¾ **cup plus 1 tablespoon semisweet chocolate chips**
- 1 **tablespoon brewed coffee**
- 1 **teaspoon vanilla extract**
- 2 **large eggs**
- 1 **large egg white**
- 10 **fresh strawberry halves, optional**

1. In a small saucepan, combine ¾ cup sugar, cocoa, flour and salt. Gradually stir in water. Bring to a boil; cook and stir for 2 minutes or until thickened. Remove from the heat; stir in the chocolate chips, coffee and vanilla until smooth. Transfer to a large bowl.

2. In another bowl, beat eggs and egg white until slightly thickened. Gradually add the remaining sugar, beating until thick and lemon-colored. Fold into chocolate mixture.

3. Transfer to ten 4-oz. ramekins coated with cooking spray. Place the ramekins in a baking pan; add 1 in. of boiling water to pan. Bake, uncovered, at 350° for 20-25 minutes or just until centers are set. Garnish with strawberry halves if desired. Serve immediately.

BAKING MORSELS

DESSERT PIZZA

I created this after my dad said that my graham cracker crust should be topped with dark chocolate and pecans. It's simple to customize this treat—just add your favorite toppings. Dad thinks the whole world should know about this pizza.

—**KATHY RAIRIGH** MILFORD, IN

PREP: 10 MIN. • **BAKE:** 10 MIN. + CHILLING
MAKES: 16 SLICES

- 2½ **cups graham cracker crumbs**
- ⅔ **cup butter, melted**
- ½ **cup sugar**
- 2 **packages Dove dark chocolate candies (9½ ounces each)**
- ½ **cup chopped pecans**

1. Combine the cracker crumbs, butter and sugar; press onto a greased 12-in. pizza pan.
2. Bake at 375° for 7-9 minutes or until lightly browned. Top with chocolate candies; bake for 2-3 minutes longer or until chocolate is softened.
3. Spread chocolate over the crust; sprinkle with pecans. Cool on a wire rack for 15 minutes. Refrigerate for 1-2 hours or until set.

CHOCOLATE LOVER'S PUDDING

I first made this dish when my husband asked me, "Why don't you ever make chocolate pudding?" It's not too rich, but it has an amazing chocolate flavor. I love preparing this homemade delight!

—**CHARIS O'CONNELL** MOHNTON, PA

START TO FINISH: 30 MIN.
MAKES: 6 SERVINGS

- ½ **cup sugar, divided**
- 3 **cups 2% milk**
- 3 **tablespoons cornstarch**
- ¼ **teaspoon salt**
- 2 **large egg yolks, beaten**
- ⅓ **cup baking cocoa**
- 2 **ounces semisweet chocolate, chopped**
- 1 **tablespoon butter**
- 2 **teaspoons vanilla extract**
  Fresh raspberries, optional

1. In a large heavy saucepan, combine ¼ cup sugar and milk. Bring just to a boil, stirring occasionally. Meanwhile, in a large bowl, combine cornstarch, salt and remaining sugar; whisk in egg yolks until smooth.
2. Slowly pour hot milk mixture in a thin stream into egg yolk mixture, whisking constantly. Whisk in cocoa. Return mixture to the saucepan and bring to a boil, stirring constantly until thickened, about 1 minute. Immediately remove from the heat.
3. Stir in the chocolate, butter and vanilla until melted. Whisk mixture until completely smooth. Cool for 15 minutes, stirring occasionally. Transfer to dessert dishes. Serve warm or refrigerate, covered, 1 hour. Just before serving, top with raspberries if desired.

Chocolate
Lover's Pudding

CHOCOLATE CARAMEL ORANGES

Chocolate and orange always taste good together, but add caramel and the result is scrumptious! Let kids help paint the leaves with candy coating for a memorable fall treat.

—TASTE OF HOME TEST KITCHEN

PREP: 50 MIN. + CHILLING
MAKES: 4 SERVINGS

- ½ cup each yellow, green, orange and purple candy coating disks
- 16 to 20 small lemon, rose or mint leaves
- 2½ cups dark chocolate chips
- 2 tablespoons shortening
- 4 wooden pop sticks
- 4 large navel oranges, peeled
- 1 package (11 ounces) Kraft caramel bits
- 2 tablespoons water

1. Place candy coatings in separate microwave-safe bowls. Heat in a microwave until melted; stir until smooth. With a small new paint brush, brush candy coating in a thin layer on the underside of each leaf. Refrigerate until set, about 10 minutes.

2. Apply a second layer of candy coating to leaves; refrigerate for at least 15 minutes or overnight. Gently peel leaves from coating.

3. Line a baking sheet with waxed paper and grease the paper; set aside. In a microwave, melt chocolate chips and shortening; stir until smooth. Dip the ends of wooden pop sticks into chocolate and insert into oranges. Let stand until chocolate is set.

4. Melt the caramels and water in a microwave; stir until smooth. Dip oranges into caramel; turn to coat. Place on prepared pan and let stand until set.

5. Remelt chocolate if necessary. Dip oranges into chocolate; allow excess to drip off. Attach the leaves as desired. Return to pan; refrigerate until serving. Cut with a serrated knife.

NOTE *Verify that leaves are edible and have not been treated with chemicals.*

MOCHACCINO PUDDING

I like to top this prize-winning pudding with chocolate-covered espresso beans and whipped cream. Pudding has never tasted so elegant.

—MARIA REGAKIS SAUGUS, MA

PREP: 15 MIN.
COOK: 10 MIN. + CHILLING
MAKES: 6 SERVINGS

- 1 **tablespoon boiling water**
- 2 **teaspoons instant espresso powder**
- ¾ **cup sugar**
- ¼ **cup baking cocoa**
- 3 **tablespoons cornstarch**
- ½ **teaspoon ground cinnamon**
- ⅛ **teaspoon salt**
- 3 **cups 2% milk**
- 3 **large egg yolks, lightly beaten**
- 1 **tablespoon brandy, optional**
- 1 **teaspoon vanilla extract**
   Whipped cream and chocolate-covered coffee beans, optional

1. Combine the boiling water and espresso powder; set aside. In a large heavy saucepan, combine sugar, cocoa, cornstarch, cinnamon and salt. Stir in milk until smooth. Cook and stir over medium-high heat until thickened and bubbly. Reduce heat to low; cook and stir 2 minutes longer.

2. Remove from the heat. Stir a small amount of hot mixture into the egg yolks; return all to the pan, stirring constantly. Bring to a gentle boil; cook and stir 2 minutes longer. Remove from the heat. Stir in brandy if desired, vanilla and espresso mixture. Cool for 15 minutes, stirring occasionally.

3. Transfer to dessert dishes. Cover and refrigerate for 1 hour. Garnish with whipped cream and coffee beans if desired.

BAKING MORSELS

_____   _____
_____   _____
_____   _____
_____   _____
_____   _____
_____   _____
_____   _____

CHOCOLATE AND VANILLA CREME BRULEE

For a truly delicious dessert that will impress every guest, give this fancy (but not difficult) recipe a try.

—TASTE OF HOME COOKING SCHOOL

PREP: 30 MIN. • **BAKE:** 35 MIN. + CHILLING
MAKES: 8 SERVINGS

- 4 **cups heavy whipping cream**
- 9 **large egg yolks**
- 1 **cup sugar, divided**
- 1 **teaspoon vanilla extract**
- ½ **cup semisweet chocolate chips**

1. In a large saucepan, heat cream until bubbles form around sides of pan. In a small bowl, whisk egg yolks and ¾ cup sugar. Remove cream from the heat; stir a small amount of hot cream into egg yolk mixture. Return all to the pan, stirring constantly. Stir in vanilla. Set aside.

2. In a microwave, melt the chocolate chips; stir until smooth. Slowly whisk in 2 cups of the cream mixture until smooth. Transfer to eight ungreased 6-oz. ramekins or custard cups.

3. Slowly pour the remaining cream mixture over the back of a small spoon into the ramekins, forming layers. Place ramekins in a baking pan; add 1 in. of boiling water to pan.

4. Bake, uncovered, at 325° for 35-40 minutes or until the centers are just set (mixture will jiggle). Remove ramekins from the water bath; cool for 10 minutes. Cover and refrigerate for at least 4 hours.

5. If using a creme brulee torch, sprinkle custards with remaining sugar; heat until caramelized. Serve immediately.

6. If broiling the custards, place ramekins on a baking sheet; let stand at room temperature for 15 minutes. Sprinkle with sugar mixture. Broil 8 in. from the heat for 4-7 minutes or until caramelized. Refrigerate for 1-2 hours or until chilled.

VANILLA CREME BRULEE *Omit chocolate chips.*

CHOCOLATE CREME BRULEE *Increase chocolate chips to 1 cup and whisk entire custard mixture into the melted chips.*

BAKING MORSELS

_____   _____
_____   _____
_____   _____
_____   _____
_____   _____

CHOCOLATE BROWNIE WAFFLE SUNDAES

One of my best friends loves chocolate as much as I do, so I like to make this over-the-top treat for when we're playing board games or cards.

—**VICKI DUBOIS** MILLTOWN, IN

START TO FINISH: 30 MIN.
MAKES: 8 WAFFLES

- 2 **ounces unsweetened chocolate, chopped**
- 1¼ **cups all-purpose flour**
- 1 **cup packed brown sugar**
- ½ **teaspoon salt**
- ½ **teaspoon baking soda**
- ¼ **teaspoon ground cinnamon**
- 2 **large eggs**
- ½ **cup 2% milk**
- ¼ **cup canola oil**
- 1 **teaspoon vanilla extract**
- ¼ **cup chopped pecans**
- 4 **scoops vanilla ice cream**
- ¼ **cup chopped pecans, toasted**
  Hot caramel and/or fudge ice cream toppings

1. In a microwave, melt chocolate; stir until smooth. Cool slightly.

2. In a large bowl, combine the flour, brown sugar, salt, baking soda and cinnamon. In another bowl, whisk the eggs, milk, oil and vanilla; stir into dry ingredients until smooth. Stir in the pecans and melted chocolate (batter will be thick).

3. Bake in a preheated waffle iron according to manufacturer's directions until golden brown. Serve with ice cream, toasted pecans and ice cream toppings.

CHOCOLATE TREASURE BOXES

Not only is this box constructed with candy bars delightful—it's also edible! You can personalize the box lid with a conversation heart or a special message written with white chocolate or frosting.

—SAMUEL NICHOLS MESA, AZ

PREP: 30 MIN. + CHILLING
MAKES: 2 BOXES (2 SERVINGS EACH)

- 1 **carton (7 ounces) milk chocolate for dipping**
- 4 **fresh strawberries**
- 5 **milk chocolate candy bars (1.55 ounces each)**
- ½ **cup vanilla or white chips, melted**
- ½ **cup cold milk**
- ¼ **cup instant chocolate pudding mix**
- 1¼ **cups whipped topping**

1. Melt dipping chocolate according to package directions; dip strawberries into chocolate and allow excess to drip off. Place on a waxed paper-lined baking sheet; set aside.

2. Cut candy bars in half widthwise. Drizzle with the white chocolate; refrigerate until set. Dip the short sides of two candy bar halves into melted chocolate; place at right angles to each other on a waxed paper-lined baking sheet, forming two walls of a box. Dip the short sides of two more candy bar halves; attach at right angles to form a four-walled box. Repeat, forming a second box. Refrigerate the boxes and strawberries until set, about 10 minutes.

3. Meanwhile, in a small bowl, whisk milk and pudding mix for 2 minutes. Let stand for 2 minutes or until soft-set; fold in whipped topping.

4. Place boxes on serving plates. Cut a small hole in the corner of a pastry or plastic bag; insert star pastry tip. Fill the bag with pudding mixture; pipe into boxes.

5. Reheat the dipping chocolate if necessary. Dip the long sides of remaining candy bar halves into melted chocolate; adhere to a top edge of each box, forming a lid. Garnish with strawberries. Refrigerate for 10 minutes or until set.

CHOCOLATE PAVLOVA

Fresh, colorful fruit tops off this lovely meringue. It's a light dessert, so it's ideal to serve after a big meal.

—*TASTE OF HOME* TEST KITCHEN

PREP: 20 MIN.
BAKE: 45 MIN. + COOLING
MAKES: 8 SERVINGS

- 4 **large egg whites**
- 1 **teaspoon red wine vinegar**
- ¼ **teaspoon cream of tartar**
- ¼ **teaspoon salt**
- 1 **cup sugar**
- 2 **tablespoons baking cocoa**
- 1 **ounce semisweet chocolate, finely chopped**
- 1 **cup fresh raspberries**
- 1 **cup sliced fresh strawberries**
- 2 **tablespoons orange liqueur, divided**
- 1 **cup heavy whipping cream**
- 2 **tablespoons confectioners' sugar**
- 2 **medium kiwifruit, peeled, halved and sliced**

1. Place the egg whites in a large bowl; let stand at room temperature for 30 minutes. Line a baking sheet with parchment paper; set aside.

2. Add the vinegar, cream of tartar and salt to egg whites; beat on medium speed until soft peaks form. Gradually beat in sugar, 1 tablespoon at a time, on high until stiff glossy peaks form and sugar is dissolved. Fold in cocoa and chocolate.

3. Spread into a 9-in. circle on prepared pan, forming a shallow well in the center. Bake at 250° for 45-55 minutes or until set and dry. Turn off oven and do not open door; leave meringue in oven for 1 hour.

4. In a small bowl, combine the raspberries and strawberries. Drizzle with 1 tablespoon liqueur; toss gently to coat. In a small bowl, beat cream until it begins to thicken. Add the confectioners' sugar and remaining liqueur; beat until soft peaks form.

5. Top meringue with berries. Arrange kiwi over berries; top with whipped cream. Refrigerate leftovers.

BAKING MORSELS

_____   _____
_____   _____
_____   _____
_____   _____
_____   _____

_____
_____
_____
_____
_____
_____
_____
_____
_____
_____
_____
_____
_____
_____
_____
_____
_____
_____
_____
_____
_____
_____
_____
_____
_____
_____
_____
_____
_____
_____

CHOCOLATE-CHERRY ICE CREAM CAKE

I often make this ice cream cake ahead of time and keep it in the freezer, wrapped in foil, for a week or so before serving. It just needs to sit out 10 minutes before you cut into it...or maybe less on a warm summer day!

—SCARLETT ELROD NEWNAN, GA

PREP: 30 MIN. + FREEZING
MAKES: 12 SERVINGS

- 1½ cups Oreo cookie crumbs (about 15 cookies)
- 2 tablespoons butter, melted
- 4 cups cherry ice cream, softened if necessary
- 8 Oreo cookies, coarsely chopped
- 1 cup (6 ounces) miniature semisweet chocolate chips, divided
- 4 cups fudge ripple ice cream, softened if necessary
  Sweetened whipped cream, optional
- 12 fresh sweet cherries

1. Preheat oven to 350°. In a small bowl, mix cookie crumbs and butter. Press onto bottom and 1 in. up sides of a greased 9-in. springform pan. Bake 8-10 minutes or until firm. Cool on a wire rack.

2. Spread cherry ice cream into crust; freeze, covered, until firm. Layer with chopped cookies and ½ cup chocolate chips. Spread fudge ripple ice cream over chocolate chips. Sprinkle with remaining chocolate chips. Freeze, covered, 8 hours or until firm.

3. Remove the cake from freezer 10 minutes before serving; carefully loosen sides from pan with a knife. Remove rim from pan. If desired, serve with whipped cream. Top with cherries.

Chocolate-Cherry
Ice Cream Cake

Hazelnut
Mocha Coffee

Chocolate
· Sips & Snacks

HAZELNUT MOCHA COFFEE

I make this frosty coffee drink for special occasions. You can make the chocolate mixture a couple days in advance. When you're ready to serve it, simply brew the coffee and whip the chocolate.

—MARY LEVERETTE COLUMBIA, SC

PREP: 5 MIN. • **COOK:** 10 MIN. + CHILLING
MAKES: 6 SERVINGS

- 4 **ounces semisweet chocolate, chopped**
- 1 **cup heavy whipping cream**
- ⅓ **cup sugar**
- ½ **teaspoon ground cinnamon**
- 2 **tablespoons hazelnut liqueur**
- 4½ **cups hot brewed coffee**
  Sweetened whipped cream, optional

1. Place the chocolate in a small bowl. In a small saucepan, bring cream just to a boil. Add sugar and cinnamon; cook and stir until sugar is dissolved. Pour over chocolate; stir with a whisk until smooth. Stir in liqueur.

2. Cool to room temperature, stirring occasionally. Refrigerate, covered, until cold. Beat just until soft peaks form, about 15 seconds (do not overbeat). For each serving, spoon ¼ cup into mugs. Top with ¾ cup coffee; stir to dissolve. Top with whipped cream if desired.

KEEP COFFEE WARM

The flavor of coffee begins to diminish within an hour after it's made. To keep coffee fresh and hot, transfer it to a carafe or thermos that's been preheated with hot water until you're ready to use or drink the coffee.

BAKING MORSELS

CHOCOLATE EGGNOG

I was never an eggnog fan—until I came up with this version! One sip of this beverage and you'll love eggnog forever, too.

—DEBBIE HOLCOMBE BRUNSWICK, GA

PREP: 15 MIN.
COOK: 15 MIN. + CHILLING
MAKES: 12 SERVINGS (⅔ CUP EACH)

- 6 **large eggs**
- ⅔ **cup sugar**
- 4 **cups 2% chocolate milk, divided**
- 3 **cups chocolate ice cream**
- 1 **teaspoon vanilla extract**
- ½ **teaspoon ground nutmeg**
- 1 **cup heavy whipping cream**
  Optional toppings: whipped cream, ground nutmeg and/or chocolate curls

1. In a small heavy saucepan, whisk eggs and sugar until blended; stir in 2 cups chocolate milk. Cook and stir over medium heat for 12-15 minutes or until mixture is just thick enough to coat a spoon and a thermometer reads at least 160°. Do not allow to boil. Immediately transfer to a large bowl.
2. Stir in the ice cream, vanilla and nutmeg until blended. Add remaining chocolate milk. In a small bowl, beat cream until soft peaks form; stir into eggnog mixture. Transfer to a pitcher.
3. Refrigerate, covered, until cold. Stir just before serving. If desired, serve with toppings.

TIRAMISU SNACK MIX

Tiramisu is one of my favorite desserts, so I took that same great flavor combination and transformed it into this fun-to-eat snack mix.

—PRISCILLA YEE CONCORD, CA

PREP: 15 MIN. + CHILLING
MAKES: 8 CUPS

- 6 **cups Chocolate Chex**
- 1 **can (6 ounces) salted roasted almonds**
- 6 **ounces white baking chocolate, chopped**
- 2 **teaspoons shortening, divided**
- 2 **teaspoons instant espresso powder**
- ⅓ **cup semisweet chocolate chips**

1. Place the cereal and almonds in a large bowl; set aside.
2. In a microwave, melt the white chocolate and 1 teaspoon shortening; stir in espresso powder until smooth. Pour over the cereal mixture and toss to coat.
3. In a microwave, melt chocolate chips and remaining shortening; stir until smooth. Drizzle over cereal mixture and toss to coat. Spread onto waxed paper-lined baking sheets.
4. Refrigerate until set. Store in an airtight container.

CARAMEL NUT-CHOCOLATE POPCORN CONES

PREP: 1 HOUR + COOLING
MAKES: 1 DOZEN

ICE CREAM CONES
- 1 **cup (6 ounces) semisweet chocolate chips**
- ¼ **cup heavy whipping cream**
- 12 **ice cream sugar cones**

CARAMEL CORN
- 7 **cups air-popped popcorn**
- ½ **cup semisweet chocolate chips**
- ¼ **cup chopped pecans**
- 25 **caramels**
- 2 **tablespoons heavy whipping cream**
- ⅛ **teaspoon salt**

TOPPING
- 5 **caramels**
- 2 **teaspoons heavy whipping cream, divided**
- ¼ **cup semisweet chocolate chips**
- ¼ **cup chopped pecans**

1. Tightly cover a large roasting pan that is at least 3 in. deep with two layers of heavy-duty foil. Poke 12 holes, about 2 in. apart, in the foil to hold ice cream cones; set aside.

2. In a microwave-safe bowl, melt chocolate chips and cream; stir until smooth. Spoon about 2 teaspoons inside each cone, turning to coat. Dip rims of cones into chocolate, allowing excess chocolate to drip into bowl. Place cones in prepared pan. Let stand until chocolate is set.

3. Meanwhile, place the popcorn, chocolate chips and pecans in a large bowl; set aside.

4. In a microwave, melt the caramels, cream and salt on high for 2 minutes, stirring occasionally until smooth.

Pour over popcorn mixture and toss to coat.

5. Using lightly greased hands, fill cones with popcorn mixture. Shape popcorn into a 2-in.-diameter ball on top of cones, pressing down until popcorn mixture is firmly attached to cones.

6. For topping, place caramels and 1 teaspoon cream in a small microwave-safe bowl. Microwave on high at 20-second intervals until caramels are melted; stir until smooth. Drizzle over cones.

7. Microwave chocolate chips and remaining cream until smooth. Drizzle over cones. Immediately sprinkle with pecans. Let stand until set. Place in bags and fasten with twist ties or ribbon if desired.

> These adorable treats were inspired by the chocolate-covered ice cream cones I enjoyed as a kid. These cones are even better since there is no melting or dripping. They'll go fast at bake sales.
>
> **—JULIE BECKWITH** CRETE, IL

Chocolate Chip
Cheese Ball

CHOCOLATE CHIP CHEESE BALL

Your guests are in for a sweet surprise when they try this unusual cheese ball. It tastes just like chocolate chip cheesecake.

—KELLY GLASCOCK SYRACUSE, MO

PREP: 10 MIN. + CHILLING
MAKES: 1 CHEESE BALL (ABOUT 2 CUPS)

- 1 **package (8 ounces) cream cheese, softened**
- ½ **cup butter, softened**
- ¼ **teaspoon vanilla extract**
- ¾ **cup confectioners' sugar**
- 2 **tablespoons brown sugar**
- ¾ **cup miniature semisweet chocolate chips**
- ¾ **cup finely chopped pecans**
  Graham crackers

1. In a large bowl, beat the cream cheese, butter and vanilla until fluffy. Gradually add sugars; beat just until combined. Stir in chocolate chips. Cover and refrigerate for 2 hours.

2. Place cream cheese mixture on a large piece of plastic wrap; shape into a ball. Refrigerate for at least 1 hour.

3. Just before serving, roll cheese ball in the pecans. Serve with graham crackers.

CHOCOLATE SODA

Poodle skirts may be out, but an old-fashioned ice cream soda is still a wonderful way to cool down on a warm day.

—TASTE OF HOME TEST KITCHEN

START TO FINISH: 5 MIN.
MAKES: 1 SERVING

- 3 **tablespoons chocolate syrup**
- 1 **tablespoon half-and-half cream**
- ¾ **cup carbonated water**
- ¼ **cup vanilla ice cream**

In a tall glass, combine chocolate syrup and cream. Stir in water; top with ice cream. Serve immediately.

BAKING MORSELS

PARISIAN CHICKEN BITES

When a friend of mine returned from a trip to Paris, she raved about the food she had and described one of the best meals she tried. It inspired me to create a similar hors d'oeuvre.

—NOELLE MYERS GRAND FORKS, ND

START TO FINISH: 30 MIN.
MAKES: 4 DOZEN

- ½ **pound boneless skinless chicken breasts, cut into ¼-inch cubes**
- ¼ **teaspoon salt**
- ¼ **teaspoon pepper**
- ½ **cup chopped fennel bulb**
- 2 ~~teaspoons olive oil~~
- 1 **tablespoon chopped green onion**
- ½ **teaspoon minced fresh rosemary**
- 1 **medium apple, chopped**
- ¼ **cup chopped pecans**
- 1 **tablespoon minced fresh parsley**
- 1 **tablespoon lime juice**
- 3 **heads Belgian endive, separated into leaves**
- 1 **cup (6 ounces) dark chocolate chips**
- ⅓ **cup seedless blackberry spreadable fruit**
- ¼ **cup balsamic vinegar**

1. Sprinkle the chicken with salt and pepper. In a large skillet, saute the chicken and fennel in oil until chicken is no longer pink. Add green onion and rosemary; cook for 1 minute longer. Remove from the heat.

2. In a large bowl, combine the apple, pecans, parsley and lime juice. Stir in the chicken mixture; spoon into endive leaves.

3. In a microwave, melt the chocolate chips; stir until smooth. Stir in the spreadable fruit and vinegar. Drizzle over appetizers.

FEEDING A CROWD

If you want an appetizer buffet to serve as a meal, offer 5 or 6 different options (including some substantial dishes) and plan on 8 to 9 pieces per guest. If you'll just serve apps before a meal, 2 to 3 pieces per person is ideal.

Parisian
Chicken Bites

TURTLE CHIPS

Salty-sweet, crunchy-chewy—there are so many sensations in one delectable bite when it comes to these chocolaty potato chips! Both kids and adults will be reaching for a handful.

—**LEIGH ANN STEWART** HOPKINSVILLE, KY

START TO FINISH: 25 MIN.
MAKES: 16 SERVINGS (½ CUP EACH)

- 1 **package (11 ounces) ridged potato chips**
- 1 **package (14 ounces) caramels**
- ⅓ **cup heavy whipping cream**
- 1 **package (11½ ounces) milk chocolate chips**
- 2 **tablespoons shortening**
- 1 **cup finely chopped pecans**

1. Arrange whole potato chips in a single layer on a large platter. In a large saucepan, combine the caramels and cream. Cook and stir over medium-low heat until caramels are melted. Drizzle over chips.
2. In a microwave, melt chocolate and shortening; stir until smooth. Drizzle over caramel mixture; sprinkle with pecans. Serve immediately.

DOUBLE CHOCOLATE MALTS

In the heat of the day, what could be more refreshing than a chocolate malt? The winning touch is the crushed malted milk balls on top.

—**TARYN KUEBELBECK** PLYMOUTH, MN

START TO FINISH: 10 MIN.
MAKES: 2 SERVINGS

- ¾ **cup 2% milk**
- 2 **tablespoons malted milk powder**
- 2 **tablespoons chocolate syrup**
- 2 **cups low-fat chocolate frozen yogurt**
  Whipped cream, maraschino cherries and crushed malted milk balls

1. In a blender, combine the milk, malted milk powder and chocolate syrup; cover and process until blended. Add the yogurt; cover and process for 30 seconds or until smooth.
2. Pour into chilled glasses. Garnish with whipped cream, cherries and crushed candies; serve immediately.

COCONUT-CARAMEL HOT COCOA

You'll think you're drinking your dessert when you indulge in this homemade hot cocoa. The decadent beverage features rich chocolate, peanut butter, caramel and coconut.

—**ROXANNE CHAN** ALBANY, CA

START TO FINISH: 20 MIN.
MAKES: 6 SERVINGS

- 1   can (13.66 ounces) coconut milk
- 1½ cups 2% milk
- ½   cup semisweet chocolate chips, melted
- ¼   cup creamy peanut butter
- ¼   cup hot caramel ice cream topping
      Coconut rum, optional
      Whipped cream and toasted flaked coconut, optional

Place the first five ingredients in a blender; cover and process until smooth. Transfer to a large saucepan. Cook and stir over medium heat until heated through. Remove from the heat; stir in rum if desired. Pour into mugs. Garnish with whipped cream and coconut if desired.

COFFEE & CREAM MARTINI

With Kahlua, Irish cream liqueur and chocolate syrup, this martini is an after-dinner specialty that's easy to mix.

—**CLARA COULSON MINNEY**
WASHINGTON COURT HOUSE, OH

START TO FINISH: 10 MIN.
MAKES: 1 SERVING

- 2   tablespoons coarse sugar
- 1   teaspoon finely ground coffee
     Ice cubes
- 1½ ounces vodka
- 1½ ounces Kahlua
- 1½ ounces Irish cream liqueur
     Chocolate syrup, optional

1. Sprinkle sugar and coffee on a plate. Moisten the rim of a cocktail glass with water; hold glass upside down and dip rim into sugar mixture.
2. Fill a mixing glass or tumbler three-fourths full with ice. Add the vodka, Kahlua and liqueur; stir until condensation forms on outside of glass.
3. Drizzle chocolate syrup on the inside of prepared martini glass if desired. Strain vodka mixture into glass; serve immediately.

BAKING MORSELS

STRAWBERRIES WITH CHOCOLATE CREAM FILLING

These party-pretty bites take just 30 minutes to prepare. Try them as a refreshing fruit appetizer.

—**LISA HUFF** WILTON, CT

START TO FINISH: 30 MIN.
MAKES: 3 DOZEN

- 1½ **ounces semisweet chocolate, grated, divided**
- 1 **package (8 ounces) cream cheese, softened**
- 1 **teaspoon vanilla extract**
- 1 **cup whipped topping**
- 18 **large fresh strawberries, halved**

1. Set aside 2 tablespoons chocolate. In a microwave, melt the remaining chocolate; stir until smooth. Cool.

2. In a small bowl, beat cream cheese and vanilla until smooth. Beat in the melted chocolate. Fold in the whipped topping and 1 tablespoon of grated chocolate. Cut a small hole in the tip of a pastry bag or in the corner of a food-safe plastic bag; insert #21 star pastry tip. Fill the bag with cream cheese mixture.

3. Place the strawberries on a serving platter, cut side up. Pipe cream cheese mixture onto strawberries. Sprinkle with the remaining grated chocolate. Refrigerate leftovers.

CHOCOLATE CITRUS WEDGES

Leftover chocolate and a lemon-themed party originally inspired the recipe. The wedges rejuvenate your taste buds while satisfying a sweet tooth.

—AYSHA SCHURMAN AMMON, ID

PREP: 20 MIN. + CHILLING
MAKES: ABOUT 1½ DOZEN

- ½ **cup orange marmalade**
- 2 **medium lemons or tangerines, peeled and separated into wedges**
- ½ **teaspoon ground cinnamon**
- 4 **ounces dark chocolate candy coating, coarsely chopped**
- 2 **teaspoons shortening**
- ¼ **cup finely chopped walnuts**

1. In a microwave, heat marmalade for 15 seconds. Dip lemon wedges into marmalade; allow excess to drip off. Place on waxed paper; sprinkle with cinnamon. Refrigerate for 30 minutes or until set.

2. In a microwave, melt the chocolate and shortening; stir until smooth. Dip wedges into chocolate; allow excess to drip off. Place on waxed paper; sprinkle with walnuts. Let stand until set.

FINDING THE RIGHT TANGERINE

Tangerines should feel heavy for their size and be free of moldy or soft spots. They'll stay fresh for a few days at room temperature and for up to 2 weeks in the refrigerator.

RASPBERRY TRUFFLE COCKTAIL

This adults-only hot chocolate is a decadent addition to any holiday gathering. If you prefer using regular milk instead of the almond milk, you can swap it in.

—MELANIE MILHORAT NEW YORK, NY

START TO FINISH: 10 MIN.
MAKES: 1 SERVING

- 1 **cup chocolate almond milk or 2% chocolate milk**
- 1 **ounce vodka**
- ½ **ounce raspberry liqueur**
- ¼ **cup cold vanilla almond milk or fat-free milk**
  Baking cocoa, optional

1. Place the chocolate almond milk in a small saucepan; heat through. Add vodka and raspberry liqueur; transfer to a mug.

2. Pour the vanilla almond milk into a small bowl. With a frother, blend until foamy. Spoon foam into mug. Sprinkle with cocoa if desired.

2. Meanwhile, in a small bowl, beat cream and cooled chocolate mixture on medium-low speed until soft peaks form. To serve, spoon chocolate cream into mugs; add hot milk and stir gently. Garnish with chocolate curls if desired.

CHERRY CHOCOLATE FLOATS

Old-time ice cream parlors may be gone, but this fabulous float will bring back as many memories as it does raves! The whole family will want to help assemble these drinks.

—*TASTE OF HOME* TEST KITCHEN

START TO FINISH: 30 MIN.
MAKES: 7 SERVINGS

- 1 **cup water**
- ¾ **cup sugar**
- 2 **cups carbonated water, chilled**
- 3 **tablespoons maraschino cherry juice**
   Chocolate syrup
- 14 **scoops chocolate ice cream**
   Whipped cream in a can
- 7 **maraschino cherries**

1. In a large saucepan, bring the water and sugar to a boil. Reduce heat; simmer for 5 minutes. Cool. Stir in the carbonated water and cherry juice.
2. Drizzle chocolate syrup into seven chilled glasses. Place two scoops of ice cream in each glass. Pour carbonated water mixture over ice cream; top each with whipped cream and a cherry. Serve immediately.

WINTER'S WARMTH HOT CHOCOLATE

I discovered this recipe as a newlywed when I was looking for something to warm us up during winter. We make it every year when we get our first snow; that's why my husband gave it this name!

—**JANINE JOHNSON** MINOOKA, IL

START TO FINISH: 25 MIN.
MAKES: 4-6 SERVINGS

- 4 **ounces semisweet chocolate, coarsely chopped**
- ¼ **cup light corn syrup**
- ½ **teaspoon vanilla extract**
- ¼ **teaspoon ground cinnamon**
- 4 **cups 2% milk**
- 1 **cup heavy whipping cream**
   White chocolate curls, optional

1. In a small heavy saucepan, melt the chocolate with corn syrup over low heat, stirring occasionally until smooth. Remove from the heat; stir in vanilla and cinnamon. Cover and set aside until cool. In a large saucepan, heat the milk until small bubbles form around edge. (Do not boil.)

WHITE CHOCOLATE PARTY MIX

You'll appreciate this microwave recipe when your oven is tied up with baking. To color-coordinate to the season, buy red and green M&M's for Christmas, red and white for Valentine's Day, pastels for Easter and spring, or orange and black for Halloween.

—NORENE WRIGHT MANILLA, IN

START TO FINISH: 30 MIN.
MAKES: 5 QUARTS

- 5 **cups Cheerios**
- 5 **cups Corn Chex**
- 2 **cups salted peanuts**
- 1 **pound chocolate M&M's**
- 1 **package (10 ounces) mini pretzels**
- 2 **packages (12 ounces each) white baking chips**
- 3 **tablespoons canola oil**

1. In a large bowl, combine the first five ingredients; set aside. In a microwave-safe bowl, heat chips and oil at 70% power for 1 minute, stirring once. Microwave on high for 5 seconds; stir until smooth.

2. Pour over the cereal mixture and mix well. Spread onto three waxed paper-lined baking sheets. Cool; break apart. Store in an airtight container.

NOTE *This recipe was tested using a 1,100-watt microwave.*

Heat the first five ingredients over medium heat in a small saucepan just until the mixture comes to a simmer, stirring constantly. Remove from heat; stir until smooth. Add rum if desired. Pour into a mug; top with whipped cream. Garnish with a cinnamon stick if desired.

CHOCOLATE WHEAT CEREAL SNACKS

Whether you eat these as a nighttime snack or on the go, the chocolate-peanut butter combo is too good to pass up.
—**TRACY GOLDER** BLOOMSBURG, PA

PREP: 10 MIN. + COOLING
MAKES: 6 CUPS

- 6 **cups frosted bite-size Shredded Wheat**
- 1 **cup milk chocolate chips**
- ¼ **cup creamy peanut butter**
- 1 **cup confectioners' sugar**

1. Place the cereal in a large bowl; set aside. In a microwave, melt chocolate chips and peanut butter; stir until smooth. Pour over the cereal and stir gently to coat. Let stand for 10 minutes.
2. Sprinkle with confectioners' sugar and toss to coat. Cool completely. Store in an airtight container.

LANDMARK HOT CHOCOLATE

My hot chocolate is a favorite beverage when the snow arrives. When the toboggan hills are calling, I leave off the whipped cream and take a thermos to go.
—**MARK PHILLIPS** BAYFIELD, WI

START TO FINISH: 15 MIN.
MAKES: 1 SERVING

- ⅓ **cup heavy whipping cream**
- ¼ **cup 2% milk**
- 2 **ounces dark chocolate candy bar, chopped**
- 4½ **teaspoons sugar**
- 1 **cinnamon stick (3 inches)**
  Vanilla rum, optional
  Heavy whipping cream, whipped
  Additional cinnamon stick, optional

BAKING MORSELS

CHOCOLATE-COVERED BACON

A hit at state fairs everywhere, this unique concoction is easy to make at home. Some say bacon can't get any better, but we think chocolate makes everything better!

—*TASTE OF HOME* TEST KITCHEN

PREP: 20 MIN. • **BAKE:** 20 MIN.
MAKES: 1 DOZEN

- 12 **thick-sliced bacon strips (about 1 pound)**
- 12 **wooden skewers (12 inches)**
- 6 **ounces white candy coating, chopped**
- 1 **cup semisweet chocolate chips**
- 1 **tablespoon shortening**

Optional toppings: chopped dried apple chips, apricots and crystallized ginger, finely chopped pecans and pistachios, toasted coconut, kosher salt, brown sugar, cayenne pepper and coarsely ground black pepper

1. Thread each bacon strip onto a wooden skewer. Place on a rack in a large baking pan. Bake at 400° for 20-25 minutes or until crisp. Cool completely.

2. In a microwave, melt candy coating; stir until smooth. Combine chocolate chips and shortening; melt in the microwave and stir until smooth.

3. With pastry brushes, coat bacon on both sides with melted coatings. Top each strip as desired. Place on waxed paper-lined baking sheets. Refrigerate until firm. Store in the refrigerator.

MAPLE HOT CHOCOLATE

When I first developed this recipe, my husband was skeptical of adding maple to hot chocolate. But after one taste, his doubts were erased. It really hits the spot on a chilly morning, especially when served with cinnamon rolls or doughnuts.
—**DARLENE MILLER** LINN, MO

START TO FINISH: 15 MIN.
MAKES: 4 SERVINGS

- ¼ cup sugar
- 1 tablespoon baking cocoa
- ⅛ teaspoon salt
- ¼ cup hot water
- 1 tablespoon butter
- 4 cups milk
- 1 teaspoon maple flavoring
- 1 teaspoon vanilla extract
- 12 large marshmallows

In a large saucepan, combine the sugar, cocoa and salt. Stir in the hot water and butter; bring to a boil. Add the milk, maple flavoring, vanilla and eight marshmallows. Heat through, stirring occasionally, until marshmallows are melted. Ladle into mugs and top each with a marshmallow.

SALTED CARAMEL & DARK CHOCOLATE FIGS

Here's a special appetizer that won't last long! Cheese, caramel and luscious dark chocolate add a delicious touch to this grown-up dipped fruit.
—*TASTE OF HOME* TEST KITCHEN

PREP: 30 MIN. + STANDING
MAKES: 1 DOZEN

- 12 large toothpicks
- 12 dried figs
- 4 ounces fresh goat cheese
- 1 teaspoon honey
- 1 teaspoon balsamic vinegar
- 1 package (11 ounces) Kraft caramel bits
- 2 tablespoons water
- ⅓ cup finely chopped almonds
- 1½ cups dark chocolate chips, melted
  Coarse sea salt

1. Line a baking sheet with waxed paper and grease the paper; set aside.
2. Insert a toothpick into each fig. Make a ½-in. cut on the side of each fig. Combine the cheese, honey and vinegar in a small bowl. Transfer to a heavy-duty resealable plastic bag; cut a small hole in a corner of the bag. Pipe cheese mixture into figs.
3. Melt the caramels and water in a microwave; stir until smooth. Dip each fig into caramel; turn to coat. Place on prepared pan; let stand until set.
4. Place almonds in a small shallow bowl. Dip bottom third of each fig into melted chocolate; allow excess to drip off. Dip into almonds and sprinkle with salt. Return to pan; let stand until set.

Salted Caramel &
Dark Chocolate Figs

HEAVENLY DRINKING CHOCOLATE

The name says it all—sipping this drink is like experiencing an out-of-this-world blend of dark and milk chocolate. The only thing to make it better? A dollop of whipped cream on top.

—TASTE OF HOME TEST KITCHEN

START TO FINISH: 20 MIN.
MAKES: 5 CUPS

- **4 cups half-and-half cream**
- **2 bars (3½ ounces each) 70% cacao dark chocolate, chopped**
- **2 ounces milk chocolate, chopped**
- **1 teaspoon vanilla extract**
- **¼ teaspoon ground nutmeg**
- **Dash salt**
- **Sweetened whipped cream**

In a large saucepan, heat cream over medium heat until bubbles form around sides of pan (do not boil). Remove from the heat; whisk in the chocolates, vanilla, nutmeg and salt until smooth. Return to the heat; cook and stir until heated through. Pour into mugs; top with whipped cream.

BAKING MORSELS

_____   _____
_____   _____
_____   _____
_____   _____
_____   _____

PEANUT BUTTER CHOCOLATE PRETZELS

Sometimes a gift from the kitchen is the way to go, like with these dipped and drizzled pretzels.

—**MARCIA PORCH** WINTER PARK, FL

PREP: 30 MIN. + STANDING
MAKES: ABOUT 3 DOZEN

- 2 **cups (12 ounces) semisweet chocolate chips**
- 4 **teaspoons canola oil, divided**
- 35 **to 40 pretzels**
- ½ **cup peanut butter chips**

1. In a microwave, melt chocolate chips and 3 teaspoons oil; stir until smooth. Dip pretzels into chocolate; allow excess to drip off. Place on waxed paper-lined baking sheets to set.
2. Melt peanut butter chips and the remaining oil; transfer to a small resealable plastic bag. Cut a small hole in a corner of bag; drizzle peanut butter over pretzels. Allow to set. Store in airtight containers.

CHOCOLATE BANANA SMOOTHIES

Get ready to make these crowd-pleasing smoothies over and over.

—**RENEE ZIMMER** TACOMA, WA

START TO FINISH: 10 MIN.
MAKES: 4 SERVINGS

- 1 **cup milk**
- 1 **cup vanilla yogurt**
- ½ **cup chocolate syrup**
- 2 **medium bananas, halved**
- 8 **ice cubes**

In a blender, combine all ingredients; cover and process until smooth. Pour into chilled glasses; serve immediately.

WONTON KISSES

These wrapped bundles are filled with a chocolate candy kiss and will delight guests at your next party.

—**DARLENE BRENDEN** SALEM, OR

START TO FINISH: 25 MIN.
MAKES: 2 DOZEN

- 24 **milk chocolate kisses**
- 24 **wonton wrappers**
  Oil for frying
  Confectioners' sugar

1. Place a chocolate kiss in the center of a wonton wrapper. (Keep remaining wrappers covered with a damp paper towel until ready to use.) Moisten the edges with water; fold opposite corners together over candy kiss and press to seal. Repeat.
2. In an electric skillet, heat 1 in. of oil to 375°. Fry wontons for 2½ minutes or until golden brown, turning once. Drain on paper towels. Dust with confectioners' sugar.

Mocha Fondue

Enticing Extras

MOCHA FONDUE

START TO FINISH: 20 MIN.
MAKES: 10 SERVINGS

- 2 **cups (12 ounces) semisweet chocolate chips**
- ¼ **cup butter, cubed**
- 1 **cup heavy whipping cream**
- 3 **tablespoons strong brewed coffee**
- ⅛ **teaspoon salt**
- 2 **large egg yolks, lightly beaten**
  Cubed pound cake, sliced bananas and fresh strawberries and pineapple chunks

1. In a heavy saucepan, combine the first five ingredients; cook and stir over medium heat until chips are melted. Remove from heat. In a small bowl, whisk a small amount of hot mixture into egg yolks; return all to the pan, whisking constantly. Cook and stir until a thermometer reads 160°.
2. Transfer to a fondue pot and keep warm. Serve with cake and fruit.

> Guests rave over this luscious fondue, which I first tried at a 25th anniversary celebration. Set out cubes of pound cake, strawberries and bananas for dipping.
>
> —**KAREN BOEHNER** GLEN ELDER, KS

CHOCOLATE SAUCE

I make my own ice cream toppings so my family can enjoy our favorite snack: banana splits. This chocolate fudge sauce is always a big hit in our sundae buffet line.
—**NANCY MCDONALD** BURNS, WY

START TO FINISH: 15 MIN.
MAKES: ABOUT 3⅓ CUPS

- ½ **cup butter**
- 2 **ounces unsweetened chocolate**
- 2 **cups sugar**
- 1 **cup half-and-half cream or evaporated milk**
- ½ **cup light corn syrup**
- 1 **teaspoon vanilla extract**

1. In a large heavy saucepan, melt the butter and chocolate; stir until smooth. Add the sugar, cream and corn syrup. Bring to a boil, stirring constantly. Boil for 1½ minutes. Remove from the heat.
2. Stir in the vanilla. Serve warm or cold over ice cream or pound cake. Refrigerate leftovers.

BERRIES & CHOCOLATE SAUCE FOR ICE CREAM

Who said an ice cream sundae can't be just for adults? I frequently make this dessert to use up juicy berries during the summer.
—**EMORY DOTY** JASPER, GA

PREP: 30 MIN. + STANDING
MAKES: 6 SERVINGS

- 4 **cups fresh strawberries, sliced**
- 1 **cup fresh blueberries**
- ⅓ **cup vodka**
- ¼ **cup sugar**
- 6 **ounces dark chocolate candy bars, chopped**
- 4 **teaspoons butter**
- ¾ **cup heavy whipping cream**
  Vanilla ice cream
  Slivered almonds

1. In a large bowl, toss berries with vodka and sugar. Refrigerate, covered, overnight.
2. Place chocolate and butter in a small bowl. In a small saucepan, bring cream just to a boil. Pour over the chocolate and butter; stir with a whisk until smooth. Cool 15 minutes.
3. Serve berry mixture over ice cream. Drizzle with the chocolate sauce and sprinkle with almonds.

CHOCOLATE GLAZE FOR DOUGHNUTS

If smooth, glossy and chocolaty is your way to glaze, you'll love this quick, easy ganache for your homemade doughnuts.
—**KAREN MOORE** JACKSONVILLE, FL

START TO FINISH: 10 MIN.
MAKES: 1 CUP

- 6 **ounces semisweet chocolate, chopped**
- ½ **cup heavy whipping cream**
- 2 **tablespoons light corn syrup**
- 2 **teaspoons vanilla extract**

Place chocolate in a small bowl. In a small saucepan, bring cream and corn syrup just to a boil. Pour over chocolate; stir with a whisk until smooth. Stir in vanilla.
TO MAKE CHOCOLATE FROSTING
Prepare Chocolate Glaze as directed; stir in 2 cups confectioners' sugar until smooth. Let stand 15 minutes or until mixture thickens to a spreading consistency. Makes: 1¾ cups.

GET TO KNOW GANACHE

Ganache is a French term that refers to the smooth mixture of chocolate and cream used for glazes or fillings. Ganache is traditionally made by pouring hot cream over chopped chocolate and stirring until the mixture is velvety smooth.

Chocolate Glaze
for Doughnuts

CHOCOLATE FRUIT DIP

My grandma helped me experiment with chocolate sauce and yogurt combos to create this fruit dip for a tea party we had.
—**ABIGAIL SIMS** TERRELL, TX

PREP: 10 MIN. + CHILLING
COOK: 5 MIN. + COOLING • **MAKES:** 1 CUP

- 1½ **cups plain yogurt**
- 2 **tablespoons fat-free milk**
- 10 **miniature marshmallows**
- 2 **tablespoons semisweet chocolate chips**
  Assorted fresh fruit

1. Line a strainer with four layers of cheesecloth or one coffee filter and place over a bowl. Place yogurt in prepared strainer; cover yogurt with edges of cheesecloth. Refrigerate for 8 hours or overnight.
2. In a small heavy saucepan, combine milk, marshmallows and chocolate chips. Cook and stir until chips are melted and the mixture is smooth. Transfer to a small bowl; cool to room temperature.
3. Remove yogurt from cheesecloth and discard the liquid from bowl. Gradually stir the yogurt into milk mixture. Refrigerate until serving. Serve with fruit.

GLOSSY CHOCOLATE FROSTING

The original recipe for this delightful chocolate frosting came from my grandmother. I lightened it up, but it still has all the flavor and richness of Grandma's recipe.
—**MELISSA WENTZ** HARRISBURG, PA

START TO FINISH: 15 MIN.
MAKES: 1¼ CUPS

- ½ **cup sugar**
  Sugar substitute equivalent to ½ cup sugar
- ½ **cup baking cocoa**
- 3 **tablespoons cornstarch**
- 1 **cup cold water**
- 4½ **teaspoons butter**
- 1 **teaspoon vanilla extract**

In a saucepan, combine the sugar, sugar substitute, cocoa and cornstarch. Add water and stir until smooth. Bring to a boil; cook and stir for 1 minute or until thickened. Remove from the heat; stir in butter and vanilla until smooth. Spread over cupcakes or cake while frosting is still warm.
NOTES *Recipe makes enough to frost 12 cupcakes or the top of a 13x9-in. cake. This recipe was tested with Splenda No Calorie Sweetener.*

DOUBLE CHOCOLATE FONDUE

Thick and creamy, this yummy dip won't last long. You can also use pretzel sticks for dipping, although I've also been known to eat spoonfuls right out of the refrigerator.

—CINDY STETZER ALLIANCE, OH

START TO FINISH: 20 MIN.
MAKES: 1⅓ CUPS

- 1 cup sugar
- 2 cans (5 ounces each) evaporated milk, divided
- ½ cup baking cocoa
- 4 ounces unsweetened chocolate, chopped
- 2 tablespoons butter
- 1 teaspoon vanilla extract
  Cubed pound cake and assorted fresh fruit

1. In a small saucepan, combine sugar and 1 can milk. Cook over low heat, stirring occasionally, until the sugar is dissolved.

2. In a small bowl, whisk cocoa and remaining milk until smooth. Add to sugar mixture; bring to a boil, whisking constantly.

3. Remove from the heat; stir in the chocolate and butter until melted. Stir in vanilla. Keep warm. Serve with cake and fruit.

MINT CHOCOLATE SAUCE

You can't go wrong with chocolate! This decadent topping seems to remind everyone of after-dinner mints. Pour the sauce over ice cream or slices of plain cake for an irresistible dessert.

—MARLENE WICZEK LITTLE FALLS, MN

START TO FINISH: 20 MIN.
MAKES: ABOUT 5 CUPS

- 2 cups sugar
- 1 cup butter, cubed
- ½ cup water
- ½ cup light corn syrup
- 4 cups (24 ounces) semisweet chocolate chips
- ½ cup creme de menthe
  Ice cream

1. In a large saucepan, combine the sugar, butter, water and corn syrup. Bring to a boil over medium heat, stirring constantly. Boil for 3 minutes. Remove from the heat. Add chocolate chips and creme de menthe; whisk until smooth.

2. Serve warm over ice cream or transfer to storage containers and refrigerate. Sauce can be reheated in the microwave.

BAKING MORSELS

_____   _____
_____   _____
_____   _____
_____   _____
_____   _____
_____   _____

HARD-SHELL ICE CREAM SAUCE

People like that this sauce forms a crunchy shell over ice cream, much like a treat from an old-fashioned ice cream parlor.
—**BRENDA JACKSON** GARDEN CITY, KS

START TO FINISH: 15 MIN.
MAKES: ABOUT 1 CUP

- 1 **cup (6 ounces) semisweet chocolate chips**
- ¼ **cup butter, cubed**
- 3 **tablespoons evaporated milk**
  Vanilla ice cream
- ½ **cup sliced almonds**

In a heavy saucepan, combine the chocolate chips, butter and milk. Cook and stir over low heat until chips are melted and mixture is smooth. Serve warm over ice cream (sauce will harden). Sprinkle with almonds. Refrigerate any leftovers. Sauce can be reheated in the microwave.

BLACK FOREST FUDGE SAUCE

I've used this velvety fudge sauce studded with cherries for years, and everyone raves about its addicting taste.
—**LINDA PACE** LEE'S SUMMIT, MO

START TO FINISH: 15 MIN.
MAKES: 3 CUPS

- 2 **cups (16 ounces) sour cream**
- 1 **cup sugar**
- 1 **cup baking cocoa**
- 1 **jar (6 ounces) maraschino cherries, drained and chopped**
- 3 **teaspoons vanilla extract**
- ¼ **teaspoon almond extract**
  Ice cream

In a small heavy saucepan, combine the sour cream, sugar and cocoa. Cook and stir over medium-low heat until sugar is dissolved and mixture is smooth. Stir in cherries and extracts. Serve warm over ice cream. Refrigerate leftovers.

CARAMEL-TOFFEE APPLE DIP

START TO FINISH: 15 MIN.
MAKES: 4¼ CUPS

- 1 **carton (12 ounces) whipped cream cheese**
- 1¼ **cups caramel apple dip**
- 1 **package (8 ounces) milk chocolate English toffee bits**
  Apple wedges

Spread cream cheese into a serving dish. Layer with apple dip and sprinkle with toffee bits. Serve with apple wedges.

The outer circle of apples around this dip makes for a very festive, eye-catching piece. It's always a top recipe request every fall for social events.

—**ANGIE HILLMAN** COTTONWOOD, AZ

CHOCOLATE GANACHE

This satin-smooth chocolate glaze will bring a touch of elegance to even the simplest dessert. It's so versatile!

—*TASTE OF HOME* **TEST KITCHEN**

PREP: 15 MIN. + CHILLING
MAKES: 1¼ CUPS

- 1 **cup (6 ounces) semisweet chocolate chips**
- ⅔ **cup heavy whipping cream**

1. Place chocolate chips in a small bowl. In a small saucepan, bring cream just to a boil. Pour over chocolate; whisk until smooth.

2. For a pourable ganache, cool, stirring occasionally, until mixture reaches 85°-90° and is slightly thickened, about 40 minutes. Pour over cake, allowing some to drape down the sides. Spread ganache with a spatula if necessary to evenly coat, working quickly before it thickens. Let stand until set.

3. For spreadable ganache, chill, stirring occasionally, until mixture reaches a spreading consistency. Spread over cake.

WHITE CHOCOLATE GANACHE
Substitute 6 ounces chopped white baking chocolate for the chocolate chips. Proceed as directed.

CRUMB-FREE FROSTING

Want to avoid getting crumbs in a cake's ganache or frosting? Be certain your cake is thoroughly cooled before frosting it.

ORANGE FUDGE SAUCE

Ice cream lovers will scream for a jar of this rich topping with a touch of orange. It can be served warm over pound or angel food cake, too.

—**ANNIE RUNDLE** MUSKEGO, WI

START TO FINISH: 15 MIN.
MAKES: 3 CUPS

- 24 **ounces bittersweet chocolate, chopped**
- 1 **cup heavy whipping cream**
- ¼ **cup butter**
- ¼ **cup thawed orange juice concentrate**
- 2 **teaspoons grated orange peel**
  Vanilla ice cream, optional

1. In a heavy saucepan, combine chocolate, cream, butter and orange juice concentrate. Cook and stir over medium-low heat until smooth.

2. Stir in orange peel. Serve warm with ice cream or transfer to covered jars and refrigerate.

Chocolate
Caramel Fondue

CHOCOLATE CARAMEL FONDUE

I only need three ingredients and 10 minutes to whip up this instant party favorite. I serve it in punch cups so guests can carry it on a dessert plate with their choice of fruit, pretzels and other dippers.

—CHERYL ARNOLD LAKE ZURICH, IL

START TO FINISH: 10 MIN. • **MAKES:** 2½ CUPS

- 1 can (14 ounces) sweetened condensed milk
- 1 jar (12 ounces) caramel ice cream topping
- 3 ounces unsweetened chocolate, chopped
  Assorted fresh fruit and/or pretzels

In a small saucepan, combine milk, caramel topping and chocolate; cook and stir over low heat until blended and heated through. Transfer to a heated fondue pot; keep warm. Serve with fruit and/or pretzels for dipping.

CHOCOLATE MOUSSE FROSTING

Although cake lovers will certainly enjoy this fluffy frosting, I also like to serve a big scoop of it in a parfait glass with cubed angel food cake or fresh fruit and topped with additional whipped topping.

—KIM VAN RHEENEN MENDOTA, IL

START TO FINISH: 10 MIN. • **MAKES:** 3½ CUPS

- 1 cup cold fat-free milk
- 1 package (1.4 ounces) sugar-free instant chocolate fudge pudding mix
- 1 carton (8 ounces) frozen reduced-fat whipped topping, thawed
- 1 prepared angel food cake

In a bowl, beat milk and pudding mix on low speed for 2 minutes. Fold in whipped topping. Frost the cake.

BAKING MORSELS

General Index

· Alphabetical Index ·